ILLINOIS REBELS

ILLINOIS REBELS

A CIVIL WAR UNIT HISTORY OF G COMPANY
FIFTEENTH TENNESSEE REGIMENT
VOLUNTEER INFANTRY

The Story of the Confederacy's Southern
Illinois Company

Men from Marion and Carbondale

ED GLEESON

Foreword by Bruce Allardice

Illustrations and Cover Design by Michael White

GUILD PRESS OF INDIANA
Carmel, Indiana

GUILD PRESS OF INDIANA, INC.
345 Gradle Drive
Carmel, Indiana 46032

Library of Congress
Catalog Card Number 96-78247

Hardcover ISBN 1-878208-88-8
Paperback ISBN 1-878208-89-6

Printed in the United States

═══A Tribute═══
To the Modern Illinois Rebels

Sons of Confederate Veterans, Illinois Division

Camp Douglas Memorial .... Camp No. 1507 .... Chicago

Pvt. John Kempshall .... Camp No. 1534 .... Maroa

Lt. Col. William H. Fulkerson ..... Camp No. 1659 .... Jerseyville

Lt. Col. Thorndike Brooks .... Camp No. 1686 .... Vandalia

Maj. Gen. Bushrod R. Johnson .... Camp No. 1718 .... Granite City

Contents

Illustrations

Maps

Photographs

Foreword

In the early days of America's War Between the States, a prominent Ohio Democrat politician, like most of his fellow party members hostile to both abolitionists and the Republican Party, threatened Union General Jacob D. Cox that 200,000 Democrats would rise up and fight the Northern invaders if the North attempted to invade the South.

The South's firing on Fort Sumter in April of 1861, and President Lincoln's subsequent call for volunteers to suppress the rebellion, put an end to any notion of serious armed resistance in the North to the war effort. The firing of the cannon largely silenced the numerous minority in each non-slave state that had always sided with the South in the pre-war sectional disputes. Many experienced an immediate conversion; Democrats by the tens of thousands volunteered for the army. Others, unwilling to kill their fellow Americans and, in a partisan sense, not at all willing to fight in a war they viewed as started by a sectional, abolitionist "Black Republican" faction, avoided any outward show of resistance to the war and kept their feelings to themselves. They echoed the words of an editor of a Joliet, Illinois, newspaper, who proclaimed, "As Democrats, we claim exemption from service in this Black Republican war."

Southern Illinois, the area known as "Egypt" because of the annual spring rises of the Mississippi and Ohio Rivers that, like the Nile River of Egypt, flood the low-lying adjoining farmlands, had been almost exclusively settled by pioneers from the upper tier of slave states (Virginia, Kentucky and Tennessee). In 1860, many of the counties of Egypt had voted by overwhelming three-to-one margins against Abraham Lincoln and the Republicans. Some of the earlier settlers had brought slaves with them to Illinois. Many inhabitants had owned slaves before moving to Illinois. Most had close relatives who lived in the slave states and joined the Confederate army. In addition to blood, geography bound Egypt to the south. Cairo, the unofficial capitol of Egypt, lies South of Richmond, Virginia. Egypt was by a large margin the southernmost area of any free state lying east of the Mississippi River, on a parallel with Kentucky and Virginia. The area's commercial contacts were mainly with its Southern sisters in the Mississippi River valley. The prewar attitude of the residents of Egypt were summed up by the editor of the Cairo *Gazette*, who on December 6, 1860, observed that "the sympathies of our people are mainly with the South."

Author Ed Gleeson has always been fascinated by the "unusual" Confederate, the man in gray who did not fit the stereotype of the Southern soldier as Protestant, Anglo-Saxon farm dweller. His book on the 10th Tennessee Infantry, *Rebel Sons of Erin*, highlighted the history of a hard-fighting, hard-drinking bunch of Irish Catholic Confederates fighting for an identity, a self-respect often denied them by their fellow Southerners, and a cause they believed in. With *Illinois Rebels* he relates the little-known story of Northern men taking their opposition to a "Black Republican" war to its logical extreme: a company of Illinoisans from Egypt who broke through the Union lines to fight for the South. In these pages we find the often humorous tale of Company G of the 15th Tennessee Infantry, the "Southern Illinois" company, from its well-lubricated beginnings in a Southern Illinois tavern to its dissolution in late 1862. *Illinois Rebels* traces the formation and war record of the only company in the Confederate army officially designated with the name of a free state. The book also serves as a mini-history of the 15th Tennessee (a regiment that contained more than the usual share of quirky individuals), in camp and in the battles of Belmont, Shiloh, and Perryville.

Illinois Rebels is not your typical Civil War unit history. Company G of the 15th Tennessee was not your typical unit.

> Bruce S. Allardice
> Des Plaines, Illinois
> Author, *More Generals in Gray*

Preface

On Thursday, November 7, 1861, one of the war's first battles on the Western front was fought at Belmont, Missouri, directly across the Mississippi River from the Confederate garrison at Columbus, Kentucky. Early that afternoon gray-clad Brigadier General Frank Cheatham instructed acting Lieutenant Colonel Robert C. Tyler to advance the men of his Fifteenth Tennessee Infantry south through a wooded area toward the blue-clad enemy.

Caught by surprise when the Rebels emerged from the woods was the vanguard of the Thirty-First Illinois Infantry, a Yankee unit commanded by Colonel John A. "Black Jack" Logan, the former congressman of Illinois' Ninth District, consisting of the lower counties of the state, sometimes referred to as Egypt. Logan, a native of Murphysboro in Jackson County, had recently moved his residency from Carbondale in Jackson County to Marion in Williamson County. The men of the Thirty-First all came from Southern Illinois, especially Williamson County.

Company G of the Fifteenth Tennessee, sometimes characterized as the Confederate Army's Southern Illinois Company, also consisted of men from Egypt, especially Williamson County. In fact the sister of First Lieutenant Hibert A. "Hibe" Cunningham, another resident of Marion, was married to Logan. It was a case of brother-in-law versus brother-in-law.

The two opposing regiments fired their opening volleys. This was an event believed to have been unique in the annals of American military history. Illinois soldiers, all from Egypt, faced each other in formal combat.

Acknowledgments

My deepest appreciation goes to Bruce Allardice of Des Plaines, Illinois, lawyer, author of *More Generals In Gray*, and member of the Chicago Civil War Round Table, for his review of the manuscript and for all of his kind assistance, especially in regards to the elusive Robert C. Tyler. A special word of thanks is due to Dr. John Y. Simon of Carbondale, Illinois, award-winning U. S. Grant biographer and professor of American History at Southern Illinois University, for his comments and suggestions, as well as for his additional postwar information concerning Thorndike Brooks.

Many thanks to Hilbert G. "Hilb" Cunningham of Metropolis, Illinois, and to his cousins, Henry and Horace Cunningham, all descendants of Hibert A. "Hibe" Cunningham, for their loan of the Frank Metcalf papers. My appreciation extends to Andrew C. Wilson of Ottawa, Illinois, past commander of the Illinois Division of the Sons of Confederate Veterans, for introducing me to this project. Thanks also to another of my fellow compatriots from the Illinois SCV, Dennis A. Stroughmatt of Albion, Illinois, commander of the Lieutenant Colonel Thorndike Brooks Camp in Vandalia, Illinois, for his information about the Southern Illinoisans in Kentucky Confederate units, as found in the introduction to this book.

Sincere thanks to the staff of the state library in Springfield, Illinois, and to the staffs of the Williamson County Historical Society in Marion, Illinois, the Jackson County Historical Society in Murphysboro, Illinois, and especially to the staff of the Oak Lawn (Illinois) Library for use of *Army Official Records*. Personal thanks to my secretary, Jeanette Nicholas of Bridgeview, Illinois, for her many valuable services.

So that those living outside of the state of Illinois will not be neglected, I hereby wish to express my gratitude to Dr. Nat Hughes, Jr., of Chattanooga, Tennessee, author of many outstanding Civil War works, for providing additional references for both the Fifteenth and Second (Walker's) Tennessee Infantry Regiments. I am also grateful to Michael Countess, a xii

research historian from Hendersonville, Tennessee, for the military service records out of the Tennessee State Library and Archives, Nashville, Tennessee; and to Susan Hormuth, a research historian from Washington, D.C., for the various records out of the Library of Congress and the National Archives and Records Administration.

Introduction

Exactly 259,147 Illinois men volunteered for Illinois state units in Illinois President Abraham Lincoln's Provisional Union Army. Exactly thirty-four Illinois men volunteered for Tennessee state units that would eventually be transferred to Mississippi President Jefferson Davis' "Provisional Army of the Confederate States" (PACS). At the risk of a monumental understatement it can be firmly stated here that the Civil War record of the former is better known than that of the latter.

The thirty-four Confederates in question were exclusively residents of two Southern Illinois counties—Williamson (town of Marion) and Jackson (town of Carbondale). Leaving their families behind, these transplanted Southerners broke out of the "Land of Lincoln" and travelled south through Western Kentucky, where they picked up more volunteers until they reached the West Tennessee recruitment camp at Union City, eventually becoming attached to the Fifteenth Tennessee Infantry, a predominantly West Tennessee regiment out of Memphis and surrounding Shelby County.

This is not to say that these thirty-four men were the only residents of Egypt (generally speaking, the bottom one hundred and fifty miles of Illinois from the town of Vandalia on the north to the town of Cairo on the south) to volunteer for Confederate service. Other small groups and individuals, mostly from the eighteen southernmost counties of the state, especially from the slave-trading community of Cairo in Alexander County, went south to fight, registering in C and G Companies of the Tenth Kentucky Cavalry. Company I of the Third Kentucky Infantry contained some native Kentuckians from Mount Vernon, Illinois. Captain Edmund W. Rucker's Battery E of the First Tennessee Heavy Artillery Regiment, known as "The Stewart Invincibles," was first organized at New Madrid, Missouri, in May of 1861. These gunners were residents of the Mississippi River towns of Southern Illinois, Southeast Missouri,

Western Kentucky, and West Tennessee. These other units consisting of some Southern Illinoisans not withstanding, however, G Company of the Fifteenth Tennessee was the only Confederate unit to be identified in army inspection reports as a Southern Illinois outfit in any battalion or regiment, as well as the only *Southern Illinois* company to be *originally* registered in a state unit from any one of the eleven seceding states of the Southern Confederacy.

The other sixty-five of the ninety-nine men who enlisted for the "Southern Illinois Company" were from Western Kentucky, Middle Tennessee, East Tennessee, Pennsylvania, Missouri, and Minnesota! Birthplaces included Canada, Ireland, Ohio, Indiana, and Illinois. Not only was this a company within a West Tennessee regiment that had not a single West Tennessee soldier, but the vast majority of the men (ninety-two out of ninety-six) were born in states other than the ones they registered from. (The birthplaces of three of the men remain unknown.) In this respect G Company was one of the most atypical units on the Southern side of the War Between the States. Of the ninety-nine men fifty-five were engaged in combat but thirty-five of them were casualties, a staggering sixty percent. In this respect the company was all too typical of units in Southern service.

Since no previous unit history has ever been written about the Fifteenth Tennessee, this book can serve not only as a Southern Illinois squadron (platoon) and company history but also as a regimental history—up to that point on June 6, 1863, when G Company was dissolved and the Fifteenth was consolidated with the Thirty-Seventh Tennessee Infantry. Information about the small Fifteenth/Thirty-Seventh Tennessee Consolidated Infantry regiment during the Chattanooga and Atlanta campaigns can be found in Captain Ed Porter Thompson's nineteenth century work, *A History of the Orphan Brigade 1861–1865*.

Readers not familiar with the main Confederate Western army (named officially in 1863 as the Army of Tennessee) may incorrectly assume that the Fifteenth Tennessee Infantry suffered heavier-than-usual losses. This is not the case. In spite of the fact that the Fifteenth could muster a mere two hundred and fifty officers and men for the October 8, 1862, Battle of Perryville, Kentucky, these low numbers were, unfortunately for the Southern cause, very much typical of Confederate Western units.

There are historical reasons for this. Thousands of Southerners were captured as the result of the unnecessary and disastrous surrender of Fort Donelson, Tennessee, on February 16, 1862. Less than two months later (April 6–7) another disaster struck at Shiloh, Tennessee, a stunning setback that left the army with a serious morale problem that led to a lack of re-enlistments and a dramatic increase in desertions. This same kind of dissatisfaction did not occur in the Army of Northern Virginia until two years later, due to the early successes of General Robert E. Lee. The confidence in leadership in the East prevented the higher rate of desertions that was experienced in the West. Consequently, Western units in Confederate service became smaller *sooner* than their counterparts in Lee's proud army. It must be readily admitted, however, that the desertion rate (24 percent) in Company G was higher than the average desertion rate (14 percent) in the other nine companies of the Fifteenth Tennessee and twice the desertion rate (12 percent) of the Western army in 1862. The reason for this is obvious. The company was a hodgepodge of men from several different states and many different counties, a condition that hurt unity and cohesiveness within the unit. The good news is that the desertion rate (18 percent) for the thirty-four Southern Illinoisans was much better than the desertion rate (28 percent) for the other sixty-five men. The volunteers from Southern Illinois, in fact, represented the only truly homogeneous group within G Company. In any case this work does not seek to point blame at the deserters, but instead gives credit to the honorable deeds of unknown Southern patriots such as Thorndike Brooks, John M. Wall, Bryant W. Hudgens, Frank Metcalf, and Spince Blankenship.

The Southern Illinoisans, along with their other compatriots of G Company, fought exclusively in the campaigns of the Western theatre of operations. Facts about all ninety-nine individual members come almost solely from the most basic nineteenth century primary sources, using a combination of military service records and pension applications from the Tennessee State Library and Archives (TSLA) in Nashville, together with muster rolls, identification cards, and army inspection reports from the National Archives and Records Administration (NARA) in Washington, plus applicable Illinois, Kentucky, and Tennessee census records.

The initial two chapters attempt to give a glimpse into the lives and backgrounds of some of the men of the Southern Illinois Company, while the last three chapters try to provide an insight into their war record. The purpose of this book is to shed a little light on some of the most obscure and forgotten American patriots of the Old South.

Ed Gleeson
Oak Lawn, Illinois
St. Patrick's Day
Sunday, March 17, 1996

Chapter One
Harry Hopper Secedes from the Union

One of the many exaggerations that continues to surface in American history is the notion that Southern Illinois during the War Between the States was a hotbed of pro-Confederate activities, with Rebel spies lurking behind every tree from Cairo all the way up to Mount Vernon and Vandalia. This notion cannot, however, be supported by historical facts. In the spring of 1861 the eighteen southern counties of Illinois were, in fact, inhabited largely by farming families transplanted from Virginia, Kentucky, Missouri, Tennessee, and other slave states. Immersed in the traditional agrarian philosophy of the Protestant work ethic, these hard working sons and daughters of Dixie were overwhelmingly pro-South and pro-slavery in sentiment, as well as Jacksonian Democrats in politics. Having been separated from their Southern heartland and from their former slaves by the passage of time, these Southern Illinoisans were, however, mostly *not* pro-secession and pro-Confederate. Their hearts may well have been with the South, but their future lay with the North.

During the four-year conflict, thousands of Illinoisans from the southern counties volunteered for federal service, especially in the original Eighteenth and Thirty-First Illinois Infantry regiments. No more than a few hundred of them volunteered for Confederate service, about one-third of whom were from Alexander County (Cairo area), most of whom had been born in the South. However, if the enormously popular and influential congressman of Egypt, John A. Logan, had declared for the Confederacy, as he strongly indicated that he was going to do instead of declaring for the Union as he actually did in August of 1861, the numbers of Southern Illinois soldiers in the two armies would have been a lot more even than they were. In fact Logan could have raised the "First Illinois Confederate" almost as readily as he organized the Thirty-First Illinois, United States Volunteers. Even if Logan had gone over to the South, however, it would have been difficult for pro-Southern troops to break out of a state so completely occupied by Governor Richard Yates' Illinois State Militia.[1]

The great American calamity began officially on Friday morning, April 12, 1861, when Southern forces, commanded by Brigadier General P. G. T. Beauregard, fired on Fort Sumter, the federal garrison in Charleston Harbor, South Carolina. Major Robert Anderson, the slave-owning Union Kentuckian who commanded the fort, surrendered late on the following day after a thirty-four hour artillery bombardment, with formal ceremonies taking place on Sunday. There were no casualties during any of the firing. That bloodless encounter ushered in one of the bloodiest of all wars. On Monday, April 15, President Abraham Lincoln issued a proclamation for the purpose of organizing a provisional wartime army. Illinois, arguably the strongest pro-Union state in the West, was asked to help raise 75,000 armed volunteers. On the same day as the presidential edict the Illinois State Militia, fearful of a pro-Southern uprising along the Mississippi River, reinforced the Federal camp in Cairo. No such threat ever materialized or was even seriously planned. Cairo became the base of all U.S. Army and Navy operations along the Mississippi and a critical Union stronghold throughout the war. In hindsight the Confederates may well have been better off seizing Camp Defiance, soon to be garrisoned, instead of Fort Sumter.[2]

Cairo (pronounced "kay-row") was then and is now a Southern town, not a Midwestern town. Residents, past and present, consider themselves to be part of the "Upper South," or "Upper Dixie." During the War Between the States, Cairo, unlike New Madrid, Missouri, which was solidly pro-Confederate, was sharply divided in loyalty between North and South. Farther south than Richmond, Virginia, Cairo is a small community set amidst magnolia trees at the very bottom tip of the Illinois arrowhead, located at the confluence of the Mississippi and Ohio Rivers which today has bridges connecting the states of Illinois, Missouri, and Kentucky. The area was settled in 1818 by a group of St. Louis merchants, who thought the region resembled that of the Egyptian city, especially when it came to frequent flooding. A prosperous little antebellum steamboat town, Cairo in 1861 was the unofficial capital of an imaginary land, Egypt, extending directly north from Alexander County to the lakes and farmlands of Jackson County and northeast to the forests of Williamson County. The area increased in prosperity during the 1850s when the towns of Vandalia, Carbondale and Cairo were all linked by rail to the city of Chicago. Southern Illinois became a gateway to the American heartland by both river and railroad.[3]

On April 29, 1861, the ten companies of Illinois militiamen in and around the newly constructed Fort Defiance, were federalized as the Tenth Illinois Infantry Regiment, United States Volunteers, a unit that was registered for three months of service. The colonel was Benjamin Mayberry Prentiss, a Virginia-born resident of Quincy, Illinois, who was a direct descendent of one of the settlers from the *Mayflower.* Colonel Prentiss' military district within the Federal Department of Missouri consisted of all of Egypt with headquarters at Cairo. His duties were to train and drill his regiment, recruit new companies, and receive reinforcements from Springfield while awaiting future reassignment. With Prentiss in firm control of Fort Defiance and most of Southern Illinois, there were not many opportunities for Confederate sympathizers to band together. One man, however, was apparently not all that impressed by the show of strength from federal and state authorities. Unfortunately for the South that one man was *not* Congressman John A. Logan.[4]

Henry C. "Harry" Hopper, a Williamson County, Tennessee-born telegraph operator and resident of Williamson County, Illinois, was a thirty-seven-year-old widower with five children, and totally unenthusiastic about fellow-Illinoisan Abe Lincoln's April 15 proclamation. Without the need of any advice or consent from a legislative body, Harry Hopper issued his own proclamation that same afternoon and nailed it to the Williamson County courthouse in Marion, a town that boasted considerable "secession spirit." The document called for a meeting to take place that very evening at 8:00 in a prominent Marion saloon. Included on the agenda were items such as resistance to Federal recruitment, recognition of Southern Independence, promoting states rights' legislation in Springfield, and preparing a movement that would eventually remove the eighteen southern counties of the Prairie State from the Federal Union as the Confederate state of Southern Illinois! Harry also authorized himself to send a wire west to Carbondale, inviting the "concerned citizens" of Jackson County to attend the meeting, all the while convinced that he had the support of Congressman Logan who was in the process of moving his residence from Carbondale to Marion.[5]

Precisely twelve men showed up for the gathering, all of whom were Southern-bred residents of Williamson County, several of whom had come early, one of whom (Harvey Hays) was roaring drunk, none of whom was John A. Logan. Calling themselves the "Illinois Committee for Southern Rights," they would soon be dubbed "Jeff Davis' Twelve Apostles" by pro-Union citizens. The twelve were: A. T. Benson, Thorndike Brooks, Hibert A. "Hibe" Cunningham (the son of John M. Cunningham and the brother-in-law of Logan), John M. Cunningham (the father of Hibe and the father-in-law of Logan), G. W. Goddard, Isaiah Harris, Harvey L. Hays, Henry C. Hopper, Peter Keifer, James D. Manier, William R. Scurlock, and James M. Washburn.[6]

The two Cunninghams assured the ten others that their famous in-law, who had been so staunchly pro-slavery and pro-South in Congress, was set to recruit a Confederate regiment (the "First Illinois Confederate") as soon as he finished moving his family. J. D. Manier, as elder statesman, was elected chairman, called the meeting to order and asked for comments or suggestions. Kentucky native Harvey Hays, a thirty-three-year-old planter, rose immediately and proposed organizing a partisan ranger unit which would ride up to Springfield for the purpose of burning the state capitol to the ground. Cooler heads prevailed and Hays' proposal was emphatically rejected. Baltimore native Thorndike Brooks, also thirty-three, a soft-spoken merchant and planter, thoughtfully suggested that a Confederate volunteer company be quietly raised in Williamson and Jackson Counties in order to avoid suspicion from Federal and state authorities. The company, as part of Logan's future regiment, would then travel secretly by night and join Confederate forces somewhere in Kentucky or Tennessee, all the while awaiting the arrival of the congressman and the other nine companies of his "First Illinois Confederate." (Brooks, the son of a prominent Maryland railroad pioneer, had two brothers who would soon join the Union Army.) After some discussion the plan was voted down. Hibe Cunningham, age twenty-five, inspired by the rebellious zeal of his brother-in-law, felt that pro-Southern citizens needed to be further "aroused" before military organization could begin. The committee agreed to draw up resolutions which would be posted on the courthouse in the morning. Harry Hopper, much like Thomas Jefferson before him, was elected to draw up the document by himself, while the others adjourned for another round of drinks. Shortly after midnight Harry's resolutions were completed.

Be It Resolved:

1) *"That we, the citizens of Williamson County, firmly believing, from the distracted conditions of our country—the same being brought about by the elevation to power of a strictly sectional party—the coercive policy of which toward the seceded States will drive all the border slave States from the Federal Union, and cause them to join the Southern Confederacy."*

2) *"That, in such event, the interest of the citizens of Southern Illinois imperatively demand at their hands a division of the State. We hereby pledge ourselves to use all means in our power to effect the same, and attach ourselves to the Southern Confederacy."*

3) *"That, in our opinion, it is the duty of the present administration to withdraw all the troops of the Federal government that may be stationed in Southern forts, and acknowledge the independence of the Southern Confederacy, believing that such a course would be calculated to restore peace and harmony to our distracted country."*

4) *"That in view of the fact that it is probable that the present Governor of the State of Illinois (Richard Yates) will call upon the citizens of the same to take up arms for the purpose of subjecting the people of the South, we hereby enter our protest against such a course, and, as loyal citizens, will refuse, frown down, and forever oppose the same."*[7]

The four resolutions were passed eleven to one. When A. T. Benson cast the dissenting vote by hand, he was knocked to the floor by Harvey Hays. Before the committee broke up for the night Hibe Cunningham proposed a mass meeting of citizens to be held in the Marion Town Square the following evening at 8:00. It was agreed. In the morning Harry Hopper nailed his revised thesis to the courthouse door and sent a telegram to Carbondale, outlining the resolutions and urging the people of Jackson County to participate. (There was considerably less "secession spirit" in Jackson County than in Williamson County.) The committee was really surprised by the large turnout in the square at Marion on Tuesday night, consisting mostly of farmers from all over Williamson and Jackson Counties. Unfortunately for the Twelve Apostles the surprise was not a pleasant one. The "aroused" citizens who seemingly had come for the "pro-secession rally" were, in fact, an angry mob of Union supporters carrying gas lamps and brandishing shotguns. Peter Keifer tried to give a speech but was quickly hooted down.[8]

James M. Campbell, a Democratic state senator from Carbondale, spoke for the majority. Although he agreed in theory with much of what Keifer had said, he warned the crowd about the possibility of an army retaliation, pointing out the dangers that a military occupation posed for families, especially women and children. Campbell's speech was cheered loudly. When A. T. Benson spoke up to agree with J. M. Campbell, he was knocked to the ground by Harvey Hays. When Campbell organized his own committee, the four resolutions were overwhelmingly rejected. The series of meetings broke up with no ugly incidents reported.[9]

In regards to the original pro-Southern committee Benson was replaced by Frank Metcalf, age twenty-four, a Canadian-born Jackson County resident who had lived previously in Graves County, Western Kentucky. Metcalf thus became the only Carbondale member of the Marion Twelve Apostles. After the four resolutions of Harry Hopper were repealed, J. M. Campbell and A. T. Benson played it safe and sent a copy of the proceedings to B. M. Prentiss (still a state militiaman) at Cairo. Prentiss, who had been hearing rumors about Rebel conspirators, was pleased by the April 16 document and issued a statement: "I'm glad to see them. The resolutions of secession would have caused you folks trouble; but now all will be right."[10]

Harry Hopper and his small committee realized their mistake in calling meetings prior to organizing their fellow citizens. Another Marion Town Square gathering was scheduled for Saturday, April 27, but to the great disappointment of the organizers no one showed up except for the original twelve, minus A. T. Benson, plus Frank Metcalf. The meeting was then transferred to the saloon. Harvey Hays made a motion to "seize the money in the hands of the sheriff to defray the expenses of arming and equipping soldiers for the Southern Army." After a considerable row, the motion was defeated. Finally Thorndike Brooks' sensible suggestion of April 15 was proposed again, presented in a formal motion, and passed.

The Logan - Cunningham Connection

Major General John A. Logan (In 1864)
Commanding General, XV Corps, U.S.V.

Captain Hibert A. Cunningham (In 1862)
Commanding Officer, G Company
Fifteenth Tennessee Infantry, C.S.V.

Mrs. Mary Cunningham Logan (In 1858)
Wife of Logan, Sister of Cunningham

Assured by the two Cunninghams that Logan was fully behind the Southern cause, the committee agreed to secretly form a Confederate volunteer company which would slip out of Southern Illinois and travel south where they would eventually hook up with Logan's other companies from the remaining sixteen counties of Egypt. Brooks was elected as the unofficial "captain" with the responsibility to recruit. Hibe Cunningham was responsible for communication with their "leader," John A. Logan. All public displays of Southern partisanship were cancelled. As it turns out, Captain Brooks would receive help from an unexpected source—Colonel B. M. Prentiss, the Union commander of Egypt.[11]

Two days after the April 27 meeting in Marion the Tenth Illinois was federalized in Cairo. Grossly exaggerated accounts of a Rebel "uprising" reached Fort Defiance. In an attempt to impress his superior officers both in St. Louis (Department of Missouri) and Washington City, Prentiss overreacted and mobilized his troops. One armed company, with one cannon, was sent north along the Illinois Central Railroad to Big Muddy Bridge Depot, four miles north of Carbondale and twenty miles northwest of Marion. Another company with another cannon was ordered north by rail from Cairo to Carbondale, where it would then be transferred to Marion. But the orders got fouled up and by the evening of April 30 both units were camped at Big Muddy. Prentiss had accomplished something that Brooks and his men could not. The strongly partisan pro-Union citizens of Jackson County, especially from the towns of Murphysboro and Carbondale, were whipped into an anti-army, anti-establishment frenzy. The outcry increased when the two big guns were noticed on the train cars.[12]

The incongruity of the moment was not lost on Frank Metcalf, who witnessed the absurd drama as it unfolded. All the pro-secession commotion had come out of Marion, not Carbondale. The Boys in Blue had occupied the wrong town! Throughout the morning of Wednesday, May 1, Metcalf spread the rumor (which he knew to be false) that the "invaders" were set to fire the cannon at any moment. In reality the company commanders had no idea what they were supposed to be doing. Some officers and men were intimidated by the wrath of their fellow Illinois citizens. By midday, large angry clusters of people gathered around both the depot and the bridge, including several screaming women wielding homemade clubs. When Colonel Prentiss received a wire about the noisy assembly, he forwarded a third company with a third cannon. These latest troops were part of the reinforcements that Governor Yates in Springfield had sent from Chicago and Peoria to Cairo.[13]

By late afternoon other members of the Democratic state delegation joined Campbell in an effort to clean up the mess created by Republican zealots Prentiss and Yates. These state officials, with considerable difficulty, prevented a serious crisis by promising to have the unwelcome troops removed if the people returned to their homes. This was accomplished. Early the next morning the bizarre affair ended when Prentiss, with the approval of Yates, withdrew all three companies and guns back down to Cairo. Along the tracks some of the soldiers recalled seeing irate farmers waving their fists. Ironically, no troops were ever sent to Marion. Noticeably absent during this incident was Congressman John A. Logan, a fact that gave credence to the theory that the man was laying low waiting for the right time to declare for the Confederacy.[14]

On May 4, two days after the departure of the newly federalized Illinois troops, Hibe Cunningham and Frank Metcalf met on a wooden sidewalk in Murphysboro with John A. Logan. It was a meeting that Logan later denied ever having and that Metcalf remembered bitterly all of his life. However, all of this was after Cunningham's good reputation had been destroyed by Logan. At the May 4, 1861, informal gathering the congressman expressed his enthusiasm about the mission of Thorndike Brooks and told the two younger men that he would be joining them as soon as he had taken care of some "unfinished business." As a result of this encounter, Brooks continued to recruit in Williamson County while Metcalf began the more difficult task of recruitment in Jackson County. The date for the start of the break-out was May 24. The rendezvous point was a wooded area near the "captain's" house, just outside of Marion. Including Thorndike Brooks himself, twenty-eight men from Williamson County reported for duty. Absolutely none reported from Jackson County, not even Frank Metcalf! Aware that he needed a lot more recruits for a full company, Brooks planned to march south and slightly east on small roads to the Ohio River, cross the river into Western Kentucky and continue recruitment in the Paducah area, all the while awaiting Confederate Colonel Logan and his "First Illinois" Rebel regiment.[15]

The twenty-eight volunteers from Williamson County were: James Bell, Thorndike Brooks, W. J. Brown, Hibert A. Cunningham, W. J. Davis, George H. Dodson, John Finnegan, Henry Gifford, Harvey L. Hayes, Henry C. Hopper, Flemming Jent, Robert R. Kelly, J. C. Kyle, A. J. Lowe, Alex McKensie, A. R. McKinelley, G. L. Patterson, G. W. Perry, Calvin Randall, Ronald M. Randall, Gardner Sherman, W. R. Tinker, R. L. Walker, William Wallace, G. W. Wandell, A. J. Wilkerson, J. K. P. Witt, and E. J. J. Wortham. The Randalls were brothers.[16]

The Marion volunteers exercised every precaution in order to avoid detection from Federal and State Militia patrols. At sunrise on Saturday, May 25, with two supply wagons carrying all equipment, the twenty-eight men set out on foot along a sixty-mile straight line route away from the Mississippi River and the Union stronghold at Cairo and toward the Ohio River and friendly Western Kentucky. After the first day's slow march Captain Brooks decided to camp at the Delaware Crossing of the Saline River, six miles south of Marion. Around sunset it became obvious that another party was following the Confederate volunteers down that same back road. The men grew apprehensive. Had they been betrayed? Brooks posted pickets armed with muskets on both sides of the wooded road and sent eighteen-year-old Robert R. Kelly north into the forest as a scout. Kelly, the only Illinois-born member of the Southern Illinois volunteers, returned shortly with a big grin on his youthful face. Nervous tension was replaced by relief and then by joy. Some of the men laughed and slapped each other on the back. Frank Metcalf had arrived with five other Carbondale area men. This small band would later make a large contribution to the future company.[17]

The six Jackson County volunteers were: Spince Blankenship, P. Timothy Corder, Sr., P. Timothy Corder, Jr., Frank Metcalf, J. T. Roland, and M. V. Williams. The Corders were father and son. Williams was a sixteen-year-old with a sense of adventure.[18]

After allowing his thirty-three compatriots a few hours of sleep, Thorndike Brooks woke the men at midnight. At 1:00 on May 26 the southeastern march resumed. Some twenty-two miles, sixteen hours and thirty minutes later, with many a pair of sore feet, the men lagged behind at several intervals. The captain ordered his six youngest men, led by Kelly, to quickstep further south in order to have "dinner for thirty-four" prepared at Linn's Hotel just below the Southern Illinois crossroads hamlet of Metropolis. Bad luck finally caught up with Brooks. A cavalry company of Illinois Home Guards (state militia) was resting at Linn's. Kelly and his teenage scouts walked into an accidental trap and were captured.[19]

A guard detachment of the pro-Union Southern Illinois state troopers stayed behind with the six prisoners, while the others rode north to intercept the main body of the pro-Confederate Southern Illinois infantrymen. Good luck made a comeback on behalf of Brooks. At the crossroads junction the militiamen took the wrong turn and headed southwest down a road that led to the river hamlet of Brooklyn, several miles away from Metropolis and Linn's Hotel. Meanwhile Robert Kelly, assisted by M. V. Williams, somehow managed to escape the clutches of his guards. Appropriating a Yankee horse, Kelly rode north alone to warn Captain Brooks. When Hibe Cunningham reached the crossroads, he noted from the hoof marks that the enemy had taken themselves out of the coming "Battle of Metropolis," the Civil War engagement on Illinois soil that consequently never happened. Brooks hurried his twenty-nine men down to Linn's Hotel and, with heavyset J. C. Kyle cursing loudly all the way, recaptured his five youngsters, tied up the guards, grabbed a bite to eat, fled south into the heavy woods near the road, and hid for the night.[20]

The exhausting journey to freedom began again at 2:00 A.M on May 27. At 12:00 noon Thorndike Brooks sent the ever-reliable Robert Kelly, mounted on the Yankee animal, down to the river landing opposite Paducah with the assignment of hiring a ferryboat to meet the slowly marching command. Some of the weary marchers made it to the Ohio River at 1:00 P.M., where the smiling Kelly was waiting for them with the steamer *Lynn Boyd,* named after a Kentucky congressman who was a distant relative of Confederate Brigadier General Benjamin Franklin Gordon, later to command Brigadier General J. O. Shelby's Missouri "Iron Brigade." By 2:00 P.M. all thirty-four Southern Illinois volunteers were aboard. As the boat took off from the north shore of the Ohio, the men passed out of the "Land of Lincoln" into neutral Western Kentucky. Most would never return.[21]

At the south shore landing the Southern Illinoisans were welcomed as heroes by Paducah's Confederate community. Captain Brooks marched his men to the St. Francis Hotel where the proprietor, an Irish-born Catholic Southern sympathizer by the name of Augustine Shields, greeted the thirty-four Southern Illinoisans (most or all of whom were Protestants) like long-lost brothers. Most of Brooks' men, including Harry Hopper, had an immediate need for some sleep. Some of them, including Harvey Hays, had an immediate need for some liquid refreshments. Gus Shields wined and dined the latter group until the wee hours of the morning. Irish-American Hays toasted his ancestral home and just about every place on earth with the notable exceptions of Great Britain and the Northern United States.[22]

When a slightly hung-over Frank Metcalf rose early the next morning a "lasting impression" formed in his mind. "The hotel was thrown wide open to our company." Pro-Southern Paducah citizens came and went all morning of May 28 bearing food, clothes, and other gifts. By early afternoon, however, Brooks had his men posted on street corners searching for recruits. This continued for the rest of that day and into the following day until 10:00 A.M. Then Clare Shields, the wife of Gus, presented the Southern Illinois captain with a beautiful Confederate flag "which was [then] carried through the streets of Paducah at the head of the company." On the afternoon of May 29 Brooks' command, reinforced by twenty-one men from that area, marched down Broadway Street to the depot, where they boarded a train down to the town of Mayfield in Graves County, Kentucky.[23]

The twenty-one McCracken County, Kentucky, volunteers were: Jeremiah Ables, J. M. Childers, Samuel Cree, B. A. Dudley, E. Y. Eaker, G. W. Harrington, J. T. Hayes, Titus Holmes, Fred A. Jenkins, Calvin R. Klein, John Mason, John McClartney, W. J. Meyer, Robert Mullens, J. F. Parkhill, John Patterson, F. A. Pentecost, W. M. Sayers, David Shields, Alfred Stewart, and R. L. Wheatley. David Shields was the son of Gus and Clare, a pair of Irish immigrants. John Patterson *was* an Irish immigrant.[24]

Arriving late at Mayfield the growing unit of fifty-five men remained overnight at the Old Cargill Hotel. May 30 was devoted to recruitment. In his memoirs Metcalf made the point that there was no fanfare in his boyhood home of Mayfield as there had been in Paducah. Graves County was even more bitterly divided in its loyalties between North and South than was McCracken County. The day's efforts produced nine more men, all from the Mayfield area, including the town's young family physician, Dr. John M. Wall, age twenty-eight, who volunteered his services as a surgeon.[25]

The nine volunteers from Graves County, Kentucky, were: J. M. Betts, A. J. Dillard, J. D. Goodridge, Thomas Gowins, S. T. Jones, A. H. Morgan, John T. Saunders, J. M. Summerville, and John M. Wall. Gowins was a fugitive from justice, having escaped from Federal authorities after having been accused of murder.[26]

That evening Captain Thorndike Brooks, along with his sixty-three fellow volunteers (a total of thirty-four men from Southern Illinois and thirty from Western Kentucky), boarded the Memphis and Ohio Railroad at the Mayfield Depot for the final leg of their journey. In the wee hours of Friday, May 31, the train crossed the border of neutral Kentucky into Dixie. West Tennessee was "Rebel Country." Later that morning Brooks' volunteer company reached its destination—Union City, an inappropriate name for the West Tennessee recruitment camp of the Southern Confederacy. The town was right on the Memphis and Ohio line in the extreme northwestern corner of the state, some six miles below the Kentucky border and about twenty miles inland from Island Number Ten, Tennessee, the soon-to-become Confederate fort on the Mississippi River in Tennessee just below the Kentucky border. Expecting the imminent arrival of John A. Logan and other companies from Egypt, the captain had his men bivouac around the Union City Depot, where they awaited registration for six full days, longer than the period of time that it had taken them to go from Williamson County to West Tennessee. As it turns out the army did not quite know what to do with the one and only Southern Illinois Company. Young Hibe Cunningham eagerly anticipated the arrival of his brother-in-law, a man he greatly admired.[27]

The Upper South Western Front, 1861-1862

WESTERN VIRGINIA

OHIO

Cincinnati

KENTUCKY

Frankfort

Lexington

Bardstown Harrodsburg

Perryville

Richmond

VIRGINIA

Cumberland Gap

CLINCH-HOLSTON

CLINCH R.

E. TENNESSEE & VIRGINIA R.R.

Knoxville

TENNESSEE R.

NORTH CAROLINA

TENN. & GA. R.R.

Chattanooga

SOUTH CAROLINA

GEORGIA

0 25 50
Miles

INDIANA

Louisville

TENN

Murfreesboro

Hoover's Gap

Tullahoma

NASHVILLE & LOUISVILLE R.R.

Bowling Green

GREEN R.

CUMBERLAND R.

Clarksville

Nashville

Brentwood

HARPETH R.

Franklin

DUCK R.

CENTRAL ALABAMA R.R.

ALABAMA

Evansville

WABASH R.

OHIO R.

ILLINOIS

Vandalia

Mount Vernon

Marion

Carbondale

Paducah

Mayfield

FT. HENRY

FT. DONELSON

CUMBERLAND R.

Dover

Union City

TENNESSEE R.

Savannah

Shiloh Pittsburg Ldg.

MEMPHIS & CHARLESTON R.R.

Corinth

Cairo

Columbus

Belmont

New Madrid

Island No. 10

MISSISSIPPI R.

Jackson

MEMPHIS & OHIO R.R.

Memphis

MISSOURI

ARKANSAS

MISSISSIPPI

Chapter Two

Harvey Hays Declares War

From the first moment of it organization the Fifteenth Tennessee Infantry was not well regarded by the Confederate high command. There were at least two reasons for this. First, all three field officers were suspected of incompetency; and second, unlike most Confederate regiments the Fifteenth was neither homogeneous nor cohesive. At first conceived as an all Memphis, Shelby County, unit, the regiment had only six original Shelby County companies including the "Washington Rifles," a unit of German farmers, few of whom could speak English, and the "Swiss Rifles," an odd mixture of Europeans who were also characterized as "Germans." Also among the six Memphis area companies was an "Irish" unit—the "Montgomery Guards." Oddly enough only two of the seventy-one men were born in Ireland; most had names that did not sound very Irish. The organizer of the regiment was Charles Montgomery Carroll, the forty-year-old former assistant postmaster of Memphis, whose only claim to fame was that he was a member of a prominent Memphis family. His father, William, had been the popular six-term governor of Tennessee. His younger brother, Thomas, had been the mayor of Memphis in the mid-1850s. His older brother, William Henry, had been the postmaster of Memphis who had appointed Charles as his assistant. William Henry Carroll, a prewar militia colonel, also just happened to be a brigadier general of volunteers in the Tennessee State Army and later held the same rank in the Provisional Army of the Confederate States. Unfortunately for the Southern cause, Charles M. Carroll, like his top two subordinates, had little military background. In fact the colonel of the Fifteenth had previously served briefly in the Tennessee State Militia (1857–1858) as a recruiter only.[1]

A friend and political ally of all the Carrolls was a prominent Columbia, Tennessee, lawyer by the name of Gideon J. Pillow who just happened to be a major general of volunteers in the Tennessee State Army. In fact, General Pillow commanded the entire state army as well as the Tennessee recruitment camps, with State Brigadier General Benjamin Franklin "Frank" Cheatham commanding Camp Brown at Union City. Pillow and Cheatham both insisted correctly that every state regiment preparing for regular service in the Confederacy post ten full companies. From June 1–3 Colonel Carroll, at his diplomatic best, persuaded four captains to bring their commands into the fold of the Fifteenth. These independent companies were from various West Tennessee counties. Peace and harmony lasted for one day. Two of the captains got into a dispute with the colonel about the arrangement with the quartermaster and withdrew their companies, taking some of the regimental supplies with them. Later that same day, Captain W. B. Isler and the "Madrid Bend Guards" replaced Captain John F. Cameron and the "Young Guard" (singular), leaving Carroll with the desperate need for a tenth company.[2]

After waiting around idle for six days, the thirty-four Southern Illinoisans and the thirty Western Kentuckians were lined up early on the morning of Wednesday, June 5, for formal registration into an outfit identified as "Captain Brooks' Independent Company, Infantry, Tennessee Home Guards." Apparently General Cheatham and his staff felt that Brooks was the right man to take in volunteers who did not fit into any known classification. To the sixty-four were added William L. Baldwin and J. G. Patterson, a pair of friends, perhaps lifelong friends. Both were carpenters; both were born in Ohio; both were residents of Pennsylvania. No explanation has ever been offered as to why the two were in Tennessee enlisting for Confederate service. The least likely Tennessee volunteer of them all was the sixty-seventh member of Brooks' company—Samuel H. Graham of Minnesota.[3]

The thin Southern Illinois majority (thirty-four to thirty-three) held fast that afternoon when it came time for the election of company officers. Thorndike Brooks was elected captain, with Hibe Cunningham as first lieutenant, Harry Hopper as second lieutenant, and Harvey Hays as brevet second lieutenant. (This brevet rank was standard with all the original companies registered at Union City.) As it turns out all four officers had been members of the Twelve Apostles out of Marion, Williamson County, Illinois. It was because of these officers that the unit was then identified by the army as the Southern Illinois Company. Dr. John M. Wall of Mayfield, Graves County, Kentucky was appointed by Cheatham as company surgeon with the commission of first lieutenant. Over the next four years there would be only one other commissioned officer either elected or appointed for Captain Brooks' company. Among the original noncommissioned officers were Frank Metcalf of Carbondale (the fifth member of the Twelve Apostles to register for Confederate service) and Robert R. Kelly of Marion, both elected as sergeants.[4]

The election took place just in time for the four offices to be filled by Southern Illinoisans. At dusk the staff of Camp Brown sent eleven more men to Captain Brooks, all as individuals from the middle counties of Tennessee, giving Brooks' reinforced command a total of seventy-eight officers and men. The eleven Middle Tennesseeans were: William Cyerpit, W. M. Davis, Calvin Henderson Ferrell, Edward Gomand, John Gray, Lester Grayham, W. W. Haywood, Richard Lyle, Isreal Moore, Frank Ogle, and Horace Sherty. At the age of fifty-nine, Private Haywood, out of Nashville and Davidson County, was the oldest member of the company. (Private Ferrell, the son of Irish immigrants, would later become a bank president. In 1922, at the age of eighty-four, the Dyer County native, who in 1861 was a resident of Stewart County, responded to a questionnaire about his war service.)[5]

In the obvious absence of any other Southern Illinois units, the four officers of Brooks' Independent Company came to the realization that they needed to attach their command to one of the Tennessee regiments. There had been no word from Logan and troops were rapidly moving in and out of Camp Brown. Brooks, Cunningham, Hopper, and Hays did not want their men and themselves left behind. So this is how it came to pass that on the evening of June 5, 1861, a pleading Charles M. Carroll latched onto a captain in search of a regiment—Thorndike Brooks. The Fifteenth Tennessee Infantry was set. The men from Southern Illinois, Western Kentucky, Middle Tennessee, Pennsylvania, and Minnesota became G Company, a West Tennessee unit without a single West Tennesseean.[6]

The Fifteenth Tennessee Regiment Volunteer Infantry
Colonel Charles M. Carroll
Lieutenant Colonel James H. Taylor
Major John W. Hambleton

A Company	Men from McKenzie and Weakley Counties. Captain B. G. Ezzell.
B Company	Men from Memphis. Captain A. C. Ketchum.
C Company	(The Montgomery Guards) Irish-Americans from Memphis. Captain Frank Rice.
D Company	Men from Madison County, including Private Robert Charles Tyler. Captain John F. Hearn.
E Company	(The Madrid Bend Guards) Men from Lake County. Captain W. B. Isler.
F Company	Men from Memphis. Captain Edward McCleary.
G Company	(The Southern Illinois Company) Men from Southern Illinois, Western Kentucky, and Middle Tennessee. Captain Thorndike Brooks.
H Company	Men from Memphis and surrounding Shelby County. Captain John Bain.
I Company	(The Washington Rifles) German-Americans from Memphis and Shelby County. Captain Nicholas Frech.
K Company	(The Swiss Rifles) European-Americans from Memphis. Captain Joseph Kellar.

Early on the morning of June 6, the Fifteenth Tennessee, along with several other units, was transported south by rail to the town of Jackson on the Tennessee and Ohio line. It was to be the first day of marching and drilling for the men. In place of fundamental training, however, the day was taken up in bickering between Colonel Carroll and some of his captains in a dispute about the "uneven numerical distribution of the men in the various companies." Captain B. G. Ezzell of A Company complained the loudest. Captain Thorndike Brooks of G Company said nothing.[7]

Ezzell's unhappiness had been momentarily reversed the previous day at Union City, when his command of eighty men from McKenzie and

Sergeant Frank Metcalf,
at age seventy-one, May 1908.

Weakley Counties had been reinforced by seven new volunteers from Middle Tennessee and two from Knoxville in East Tennessee. Even though eighty-nine was better than the average number of men in the regimental companies, Ezzell got caught up in a shouting match with Carroll, claiming that he needed a full unit of one-hundred men for "deployment purposes." The colonel, highly offended by his subordinate's attitude, retaliated by pulling the Middle and East Tennesseans back out of A Company and by putting them into G Company, thereby decreasing Captain Ezzell's numerical strength down to the previous eighty officers and men, while increasing Captain Brooks' numerical strength up to eighty-seven officers and men, not a one of whom was from Memphis, Shelby County, or anywhere else in West Tennessee.[8]

The nine latest Tennessee members of the Southern Illinois Company were: W. J. Cooper, Bryant W. Hudgens, J. A. Hunter, Joshua B. Johnson, Daniel Knight, J. W. Lewelling, Asa G. Morris, Joseph Parton, and J. P. Price. Hudgens of Cheatham County, one week short of his twentieth birthday, would become the last commissioned officer of the company. The two East Tennesseans were Cooper and Price.[9]

Friday, June 7, at Jackson, represented the date and place of the official transfer of the Fifteenth from the Tennessee Home Guards to the Tennessee State Army. State records listed 744 officers and men present for duty, most armed with flintlock muskets left over from the War of 1812, a few of which could actually be fired. In late July the regiment was sent back up to Union City and from there west to New Madrid, Missouri, on the Mississippi River just above Island Number Ten, Tennessee.[10]

On July 9, 1861, the Tennessee State Army was transferred to the Provisional Army of the Confederate States. Arriving on August 1, the men of the Fifteenth Tennessee Infantry were mustered into that army for a period of one year. Also on that same day Captain Brooks personally recruited a local New Madrid resident, Leroy Wallace, into his company, increasing his numerical strength to eighty-eight officers and men and giving him to date the largest company in the regiment. On August 9 General Cheatham ordered Colonel Carroll to split his command between New Madrid and Island Number Ten. Carroll, demonstrating a preference to work with his home townsmen, kept the four English-speaking Memphis companies (B, C, F, H) with him at the Missouri river town and sent the German Washington Rifles (I) and Swiss Rifles (K) down to the Tennessee fort along with the four companies (A, D, E, G) from outside of Shelby County, including the Southern Illinois Company. While doing garrison duty at Island Number Ten from August 10 to September 1, Thorndike Brooks gathered five more recruits for his command, all Middle Tennesseans without previous units. The company then boasted ninety-three officers and men.[11]

The five newcomers were: J. L. Gryder, Bryce Holland, Joshua Lowe, James Mowlen, and B. L. Walston.[12]

On September 1, 1861, both detachments of the Fifteenth Tennessee were sent on transports up the Mississippi to the Confederate fortress at Columbus, Kentucky, where regiments from all over the South were concentrating. First Lieutenant Hibert A. Cunningham expected to find his brother-in-law, John A. Logan, as a Confederate colonel, waiting for him at Columbus. Hibe was shocked to learn that Logan had declared himself for the Union at the Marion Town Square twelve days previous. Ironically, it had happened at the same location as the "pro-secession" rally of April 27. There would be no more talk of a "First Illinois Confederate." While the Rebel Southern Illinois Company did guard duty at Columbus, Colonel John A. Logan was in the process of organizing his Yankee Thirty-First Illinois in Egypt. By September 4 all ten companies of the Fifteenth were reunited under Charles M. Carroll. Starting on the next day Thorndike Brooks began his efforts to scrape together his last six recruits—all from local Graves County, Western Kentucky.[13]

These last six men were: C. F. Carmon, J. T. Gunn, E. C. Hunter, D. L. L. McGeehee, J. M. Payne, and W. T. Pentecost, the cousin of F. A. Pentecost, who had joined up at Paducah.[14]

A total of ninety-nine officers and men had registered for G Company of the Fifteenth Tennessee Regiment Volunteer Infantry, a unit that would never benefit from future new recruits. Listed by the Richmond, Virginia, War Department as the army's lone Southern Illinois Company, thirty-six of the men were from Western Kentucky, thirty-four from Southern Illinois, twenty-three from Middle Tennessee, two each from East Tennessee and Pennsylvania, and one each from Missouri and Minnesota. Brooks' command was the largest of the ten companies of Carroll's West Tennessee regiment. Oddly enough, not one single member of the company was a resident of any of the counties in West Tennessee. It should be noted here that the ninety-nine volunteers were never in camp together at the same time. As the final recruits were being rounded up, the ranks were already in the process of thinning out due to illness, resignations, and desertions.[15]

The most notable loss occurred when likeable and highly respected Sergeant Robert R. Kelly, already appointed as an assistant quartermaster, was forced to resign from the army at Island Number Ten. In early August a letter arrived from young Kelly's extended family back in Williamson County reporting that the sergeant's teenaged bride had been taken ill. Kelly immediately requested a personal discharge and it was granted on August 18. This sad episode has a happy ending—Mr. and Mrs. Kelly both survived many years and had many children. Robert R. Kelly was replaced as assistant quartermaster, with the rank of sergeant, by the popular twenty-eight-year-old Minnesotan, Samuel H. Graham, who promptly distributed seventy-five slightly used pairs of socks that had been requisitioned by Kelly.[16]

Commanding the Union Department of Missouri in 1861 was Major General John C. Frémont, with headquarters in St. Louis. Commanding Frémont's District of Cairo, including all of Egypt, was Brigadier General U. S. Grant, most recently of Galena, Illinois, whose West Point nickname had been Uncle Sam. Frémont's Confederate counterpart was Major General Leonidas Polk, the former Episcopal bishop of Louisiana. On September 15 President Jefferson Davis replaced Polk as the commanding general of Confederate Department Number Two (the West) with the legendary Texan, General Albert Sidney Johnston. In reality Johnston merely superseded Polk, with Polk remaining as commander of Johnston's center, which most especially included the Mississippi River. Just prior to General Johnston's arrival, General Polk had made a huge mistake in judgment.[17]

Concerned about the U.S. Navy buildup around Fort Defiance at Cairo, Illinois, Polk seized the ungarrisoned town of Columbus, Kentucky, located on the Mississippi, nineteen miles below Cairo. Directly across the river from Columbus on the east bank was the three-farm landing of Belmont, Missouri, on the west bank, seventeen miles below General Grant's camp at Bird's Point, Missouri, opposite Cairo. General Polk had momentarily taken control of the Upper Mississippi while keeping a strong foothold on the soil of both Missouri and Kentucky. In doing so, however, the Louisiana resident had seriously violated Kentucky neutrality. On the same day that Columbus was occupied, the state legislature of Kentucky met, expressed outrage about the "invasion," and committed itself totally to the Union cause. Thousands of Kentuckians soon joined the Federal Army.[18]

Also on that same September 4, General Sam Grant arrived in Cairo with a new assignment. General Frémont had promoted the aggressive Northern Illinoisan to the command of an expanded District of Southeast Missouri, with headquarters remaining in Cairo. Frémont ordered Grant to accomplish two tasks. First, clear Meriwether "Jeff" Thompson's cavalry out of the district; and second, make preparations to open the Upper Mississippi by capturing and holding Columbus. Thompson, formerly the mayor of the town of St. Joseph, was the Confederate Missouri militia partisan known as the "Swamp Fox." His guerilla tactics had played havoc with Federal supply lines. Grant immediately sent out his Illinois cavalry regulars—with mixed results. Then, in a bold stroke that greatly strengthened his district, the Illinoisan sailed east and occupied undefended Paducah, Kentucky, on September 6, making Polk vulnerable to a land attack from his rear. A week later General Grant was reinforced in Cairo by Colonel Logan and the Southern Illinoisans of the Thirty-First Illinois Infantry who were mustered into the Union Army on September 18 for up to three years of service.[19]

In the meantime General Leonidas Polk, with the approval of General Sidney Johnston and assisted by Generals Gideon Pillow and Frank Cheatham, was assembling an entire army corps in and around Columbus. By late September Polk had some 17,500 Boys in Gray, mostly from twenty-five infantry regiments from all over the Western Confederacy, including state units from Tennessee, Kentucky, Missouri, Arkansas, Mississippi, Louisiana, and Texas. Among these was, of course, the Fifteenth Tennessee. In October, after having secured all of the landings on the Missouri shore from Belmont up to Norfolk and all of the landings on the Kentucky shore from Columbus up to Elliott's Mills, the bishop-general finally began to worry about his back door.[20]

The Federal presence at Paducah was a major Confederate problem.

The three Kentucky towns below Paducah along the New Orleans and Ohio Railroad line could easily be occupied by the Boys in Blue arriving on trains. From north to south the three depots were Plumley's Station, Viola, and Mayfield, home of First Lieutenant John M. Wall and former home of Sergeant Frank Metcalf. On May 29, Captain Thorndike Brooks' company had traveled by rail from Paducah to Mayfield, which had demonstrated the convenience of the route to the Southern Illinoisans and Western Kentuckians. If General Grant gained control of that same railroad, he could amass a sizable command directly east (inland) from Columbus, forcing General Polk to wage a campaign on two fronts.[21]

In order to prevent this from happening, the bishop-general sent his pioneers (engineers) over to the railroad south of Viola and north of Mayfield to tear up the track. The break-up of the railroad, like the occupation of Columbus, caused Polk to feel the wrath of Western Kentucky citizens, especially those from McCracken and Graves Counties, home of thirty-six members of G company, Fifteenth Tennessee Infantry. In order to secure his working parties, the Louisiana general occupied the two Kentucky towns between the river and the railroad—Melvin, west of Viola, and Milburn, west of Mayfield. The various gray-clad regiments rotated duty at Columbus, at the river landings, and at the Melvin/Milburn camps.[22]

On October 14, as Colonel "Jack" Logan was drilling and marching his federalized regiment at Cairo, a small force of General Sam Grant's regular cavalry mixed it up with detached elements of General Jeff Thompson's command near Bird's Point. Also on that same day Colonel Charles Carroll was given the simple-simon detail of marching his regiment nine miles east from the Iron Works at Columbus (high ground at the garrison) to the small camp just west of Milburn. Amazingly, he managed to screw up the assignment. The first formal march of the Fifteenth Tennessee Infantry proved to be unsuccessful, due to the fact that the men could *not* march. The reason they could not march was that no one had ever showed them how. In fact they did not know how to do much of anything militarily—for the same reason. The eastward advance from the Iron Works was painfully slow, and the men straggled badly. Only D Company from Madison County under Captain John F. Hearn had any semblance of order and discipline. By evening some elements of the regi-

Belmont – Columbus Area, 1861

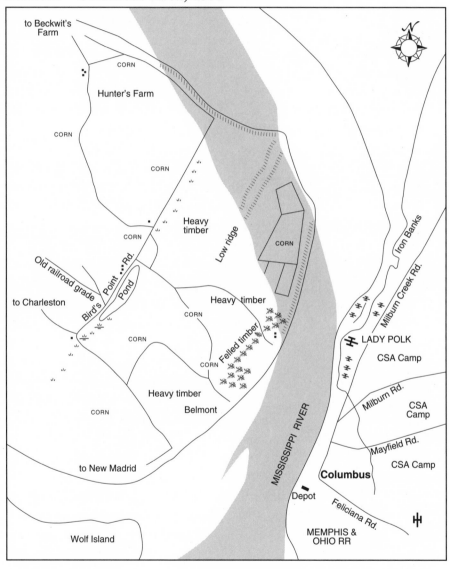

ment had gone about half the distance from Columbus to Milburn and were ready to call it a day, while other elements were still at the Iron Works.[23]

It was then discovered that the men also did not know how to bivouac, so most of them slept on the ground wherever they were. Some took the opportunity to go AWOL. In the morning the situation went from bad to worse. As some of the men began to stroll along the road toward Milburn, still others were arriving from Columbus, while still others decided to spend some time at the local farm houses. It was at this time that the men of the Fifteenth Tennessee experienced their first fighting. It was not, however, the Tennesseeans versus the Yankees. It was the Memphis Irish-Americans of C Company, the Montgomery Guards, versus the Memphis German-Americans of I Company, the Washington Rifles. In order to achieve absolute chaos, Brevet Second Lieutenant Harvey Hays and some of the men of the Southern Illinois Company joined forces with the "Irishmen," while members of the Swiss Rifles joined forces with the "Germans."[24]

The causes for the brawl on the Milburn Road are as mysterious as the "march" itself. Two facts are known for sure. First, the Washington Rifles were involved, because Captain Nicholas Frech, at a later hearing, implicated a few of his own men. Second, Hays was involved because Frank Metcalf, in his memoirs, points to Harvey at the center of the storm. It can safely be assumed that liquor, lack of communication, and lack of purpose contributed to the confrontation. Some of the men had been up all night drinking, some of the Germans could not speak English, and no one had been given any orders. Even more mysterious were the whereabouts of Colonel Carroll and his staff.[25]

Although the fisticuffs were brief and isolated, the disorganized advancement came to a standstill. For the remainder of October 15, some officers and men casually walked eastward toward Milburn, while others casually walked westward back to Columbus! By evening of the second day the ragged nine-mile "line" of the Fifteenth Tennessee ran all the way from the Iron Works to the Western Kentucky town. Observers could not tell which end of the column was the lead, a situation perhaps unique in the annals of American military history outside the context of a battle. Carroll finally surfaced at Milburn later that night and only then because he got into a reported dispute with his own top two subordinates, Lieutenant Colonel James H. Taylor and Major John W. Hambleton. At that point no one in the regiment had any confidence in leadership. On October 16 the Fifteenth, or whatever was left of it, was "recalled" to the garrison.[26]

Even the mild-mannered, gentlemanly General Leonidas Polk was upset. On October 17, Carroll was court-martialed for "conduct prejudicial to good order and discipline" and found guilty. The Memphis lawyer/postmaster was not, however, cashiered from the army. The kindly bishop-general allowed Carroll to stay on as "adjutant" of his own regiment with the same rank of colonel, an odd turn of events to say the least. (Charles M. Carroll later became a highly competent staff officer with the reduced rank of captain. The general officer he served was the best Memphis warrior of them all—the "Wizard of the Saddle," Nathan Bedford Forrest.) Taylor and Hambleton both resigned and were given other commissions. Because Carroll was still at Columbus, the colonelcy of the Fifteenth Tennessee was temporarily left vacant. But in order for the regiment to survive as a viable unit, two competent field officers would have to be selected without delay. Scouts reported that General U. S. Grant was planning some sort of "expedition." In fact, Colonel John A. Logan and the men of the Thirty-First Illinois Infantry eagerly awaited orders to move south.[27]

Captain John F. Hearn, a no-nonsense type of officer, was promoted to regimental second-in-command with the rank of major, based at least partly on the fact that his D Company from Madison County was the first unit to have arrived at Milburn intact. The officers and men of the discredited regiment knew only too well that the soldier elected to serve as their lieutenant colonel and field commander would have to be an able officer. If the process failed and the men did not shape up, the Fifteenth Tennessee Infantry might well be disbanded by a concerned general staff.[28]

Their surprising choice came from deep inside their own ranks. He was acting Lieutenant Colonel (Major) Robert Charles Tyler, age twenty-eight, an obscure Marylander with a brief residency at Memphis, who since October 2 had been an assistant quartermaster on General Cheatham's staff with the rank of major. A former filibuster, Tyler had registered in June as a private in Hearn's company. His personal efficiency became known to Cheatham who used him in several capacities. Hardly anyone in or out of the Fifteenth knew much of anything about the quiet young Tyler. His rise from private to acting lieutenant colonel in five months was one more unusual feature about the regiment. By the end of October 1861, the Fifteenth Tennessee Infantry was commanded by an original enlisted man. The original enlisted man's second-in-command was his original commanding officer. The original enlisted man's adjutant was the man who still held the rank of regimental colonel. General Polk thought the selection of Tyler to be especially uninspiring. As was the case in a number of his military judgments, Polk was wrong. In spite of his command inexperience, acting Lieutenant Colonel Robert Charles Tyler, who would eventually fight his way up to the rank of brigadier general, gradually became an outstanding combat officer. He had to prove himself worthy very quickly. Given his temporary commission on October 24, Tyler had exactly two weeks to properly drill and train his demoralized regiment in preparation for the first major battle to be fought for possession of the mighty Mississippi.[29]

Chapter Three
Baptism at Belmont

Faulty Union scouting reports led General Grant at Cairo to believe that General Polk at Columbus was reinforcing Missouri State Major General Sterling Price, commanding the Missouri State Guard (an army), by sending troops across the Mississippi from Columbus to Belmont. According to these reports Polk's infantrymen, protected by General Jeff Thompson's partisans, were then heading west into the Missouri interior to link up with Price's state troops. None of it was true. Polk at Columbus was not reinforcing Price in Missouri and Thompson was not in the vicinity of Belmont. The ambitious and aggressive Grant, however, figured that he could secure both his objectives at the same time. He would capture or destroy the pesky Thompson, soften up the defenses at Columbus by taking the Confederate camp (Camp Johnston) at Belmont, and eventually force the defensive-minded Polk out of his garrison.[1]

On November 3, 1861, Sam Grant sent a brigade under Colonel Richard J. Oglesby to do battle with Jeff Thompson's "Swamp Rats" in Eastern Missouri, while another brigade under Brigadier General Charles F. Smith was sent marching down into Western Kentucky from Paducah through Melvin and Milburn with orders to probe the Rebel defenses at Columbus. Meanwhile Grant himself would take five regiments on transports down the Mississippi, land on the western (Missouri) shore above Belmont and take Polk's observation post at Camp Johnston.[2]

The idea was for the three Federal commands to join together. Oglesby's five regiments would drive Thompson further west and then meet Grant's five regiments at Belmont. These ten regiments, protected by the U.S. Navy, would then cross the river and join Smith's five regiments in an attack against Polk at Columbus. But Oglesby would not get to Belmont on time, and Smith would not get to Columbus on time. On the morning of Thursday, November 7, Grant's 3,500 infantrymen, separated into two brigades, landed at Hunter's Farm three miles above Belmont and prepared to attack the 1,000 Confederates at Camp Johnston, while 16,500 other Confederates watched from the Iron Banks on the eastern (Kentucky) shore, protected by their huge gun, "Lady Polk." (Three of Grant's regiments, including the Thirty-First Illinois, were commanded by Brigadier General John A. McClernand of Southern Illinois, while the other two regiments were commanded by Colonel Henry Dougherty of Central Illinois.)[3]

While General Grant was planning his three-pronged expedition, Generals Polk and Pillow busied themselves by dividing and subdividing their regiments into an array of "divisions" and "brigades," each division of two brigades and each brigade of two regiments, so that on paper, at least, it appeared that the entire Department of the West was defending Columbus. The last two regiments to be brigaded were the poorest trained and least respected outfits. The Confederate "Reserve Brigade" consisted of the elderly Colonel Samuel F. Marks (age fifty-eight) and his Eleventh Louisiana Infantry, a predominantly Catholic outfit, plus acting Lieutenant Colonel Robert C. Tyler and his Fifteenth Tennessee Infantry.[4]

Marks' problem was similar to Tyler's. When the Louisiana veteran inherited his motley crew, he was shocked to discover that the men could not perform basics such as "Present Arms" and "Stack Arms" for the simple reason that the company captains could not give the appropriate orders. When the colonel was given command of the reserves, he found himself not with one disorganized regiment but with two. Fortunately for Marks, Tyler proved himself to be a cooperative and energetic young officer. An army inspection report noted that a "confrontation arose" between certain men of the two reserve regiments but, without providing specifics, also noted that R. C. Tyler quickly put an end to it.

On the same Thursday morning that General U. S. Grant landed his troops, Captain Thorndike Brooks reported seventy officers and men of G Company present for duty, which meant that he had lost twenty-nine men for one reason or the other before the first shot had been fired. The Southern Illinoisan and his men had ringside seats for the coming fight across the river.[5]

Brigadier General Robert Charles Tyler in 1864.

The meager gray-clad forces at Camp Johnston just above the Belmont landing consisted of Colonel James S. Tappan's "brigade," that is, all ten companies of his own Thirteenth Arkansas Infantry, two companies of the First Mississippi Battalion Cavalry, and the six guns of the Watson Louisiana Artillery Battalion, a Catholic unit of two batteries featuring Creole gunners from New Orleans and Irish gunners from Memphis. Lieutenant Colonel Daniel Beltzhoover, the Maryland-born Mississippi commanding officer of the Louisiana and Tennessee "Watsons," a Catholic and a stern West Point disciplinarian, had once been arrested for striking one of his own men with his sword because the enlisted man refused to return a knife to the quartermaster as ordered.[6]

At 8:30 A.M., as General Grant left four of his fifty companies (all from Dougherty's small brigade) at Hunter's Farm guarding the troop transports in full view of Colonel Tappan's Mississippi scouts, the Arkansan sent an urgent request for reinforcements across the river. General Polk incorrectly believed that Grant's 3,114 advancing blue-clads from Illinois and Iowa were merely a diversion, and that the main Union thrust would come against Columbus from General C. F. Smith's command at Paducah. As the result of this false assumption, the Confederate commander sent reinforcements over the river from Columbus to Belmont *very* cautiously. While Sam Grant marched inland, south and east, on the Hunter's Farm Road down to Camp Johnston, Gideon Pillow arrived by steamer at the Belmont landing below the camp with four Tennessee infantry regiments—the Twelfth, Thirteenth, Twenty-First, and Twenty-Second, all of which gave the Southerners the same number of regiments and almost the same number of men as the Northerners. But when the opposing forces collided shortly after 10:00 A.M., the results were anything but even.[7]

In defiance of all human logic, General Pillow marched north and posted his five regiments and six guns in an open cornfield west of Camp Johnston, the eastern and southern sections of which were not even connected to the local woods. General Grant's Illinoisans and Iowans came off the Hunter's Farm Road and out of those same woods, quickly chasing the exposed Tennesseeans and Arkansans back east through the cornfield to the camp. The Federals celebrated their early and easy victory by plundering the tents and setting fire to the camp. When General Polk observed the happy Yankees and their large bonfire from his perch atop the Iron Works, he was inspired to do something. Not exactly taking a calculated risk, the Louisiana bishop-general committed one more regiment to Belmont—the Second Tennessee Infantry. This bunch was a rowdy unit of Memphis Irishmen commanded by Colonel James Knox Walker, a Memphis politician who was the nephew and personal secretary of the late President James Knox Polk as well as a relative of General Leonidas Polk himself. Not too surprisingly Walker also just happened to have been a political associate of General Gideon J. Pillow.[8]

The Irishmen did well in restoring some order to Pillow's scattered forces, but Grant still held the initiative and was pushing further east toward the river. It was shortly before 11:00 when Polk noticed more blue-clad troops forming a line along the Missouri shore. It seemed obvious that the enemy had penetrated all the way to the western bank. Not all things, however, are what they seem to be. The men in blue uniforms were the gunners of the Confederate Watson Artillery, on the wooded bank, protecting their guns from the assault of the Federal Westerners.[9]

Like many American generals after him, Polk was determined to drive the enemy off the beachhead. In this unusual situation, however, the enemy was *not* on the beachhead. Still reluctant to allow his best troops to leave their positions around the garrison, he called up his Reserve Brigade of Colonel Samuel F. Marks with orders to clear the blue-clads off the beach on the Missouri shore. As commanding officer of the reserves, Marks was to take his own Eleventh Louisiana across the river first to be followed by the Fifteenth Tennessee. Somehow the transport assignments got switched and acting Lieutenant Colonel Robert C. Tyler's steamer, *Hill,* was ready to take off before Marks' steamer, *Charm.* With some difficulty Tyler managed to cram most of his men onto the three decks, including forty-seven of the seventy officers and men of G Company (the other twenty-three were either on guard duty or could not be found) as Captain Thomas H. Newell steered *Hill* toward Camp Johnston. As the Confederate troop transport took off from the Columbus landing on the eastern shore, the Confederate Creoles and Irishman on the western shore shouted for joy as they ran down to the Belmont landing to welcome their rescuers. This proved to be a mistake.[10]

Acting Lieutenant Colonel Tyler went all over the boat preparing his officers and men for combat by reminding them that the enemy destruc-

tion of Camp Johnston needed to be avenged. As he was making his
rounds, the soldiers in blue emerged from the wooded bank. It is not
known if any particular officer of the Fifteenth ordered the opening volley to be fired. Soon spontaneous musketry erupted from all three decks
of the steamer. The startled Creoles and Irishmen fled back to the cover
of the woods. An angry and confused Lieutenant Colonel Beltzhoover
figured that the Columbus garrison must have been seized by Federal
troops. He had one cannon moved to the landing. The first solid shot
from the Confederate gun came so close to the *Hill* that many of the
Confederate infantrymen on the first deck and some on the second were
splashed with water.[11]

Tyler steadied his officers, including Captain Thorndike Brooks, while
ordering a concentrated fire toward Beltzhoover and his gunners. The
acting lieutenant colonel of the Fifteenth Tennessee was later quoted by a
newspaper reporter to have said: "The Federal gunners directed shots at
the hull to sink her." Sergeant Frank Metcalf of the Southern Illinois
Company remembered an infuriated Brevet Second Lieutenant Harvey
Hays, who couldn't swim, firing "round after round" from his musket.
As the Confederate gun continued to throw solid shots into the Mississippi River, and as the Confederate riflemen on the boat continued to
send lead in the direction of the cannon, Captain Newell skillfully piloted
the *Hill* out of harm's way and up the river against currents to the next
landing four-hundred yards north of Camp Johnston. The men of the
Rebel battery wondered how many more Yankee troop ships would come
after them. The men of the Rebel regiment wondered if all the Yankee
artillerymen would be that tough. So this is how it came to pass that the
men of the Fifteenth Tennessee, including G Company, participated in
their first combat action against their own side, although most of them
went to their graves not knowing this.[12]

Tyler hid his ten companies on the wooded bank north of the disorganized battle and awaited the arrival of his brigade commander. Fortunately
for Tyler, Marks aboard the *Charm* had viewed the "river battle" between
the Confederate battery and the Confederate boat. As a result the Eleventh Louisiana disembarked at the same northern landing as the Fifteenth
Tennessee, ultimately giving the Belmont Confederates eight regiments
to Grant's five. For the Boys in Gray the most important change in com-

mand occurred at the top when the inept Pillow was replaced as field commander by General Frank Cheatham, the hard-drinking, hard-fighting ex-farmer from Nashville.[13]

At first it was not General Cheatham who turned the tide against General Grant. It was, instead, Brigadier General John A. McClernand, the pompous Southern Illinois commander of Grant's predominantly Central and Southern Illinois First Brigade (the Twenty-Seventh, Thirtieth, and Thirty-First Illinois Infantry) who turned the tide against Grant. Late in the morning the ambitious politician gave a premature victory speech to his celebrating troops at Camp Johnston, causing many of the Central and Southern Illinoisans to become drunk and nearly all of them to become disorganized.[14]

When Cheatham joined Marks at the northern landing, he pieced together remnants of Pillow's original six regiments, especially companies from the Irish Second Tennessee, the Thirteenth Tennessee, and the Thirteenth Arkansas. The big Middle Tennessean led this force directly south toward the northern end of Camp Johnston. He ordered Marks to go west inland from the river and then south to the woods at the western end of the camp for the purpose of advancing east against the enemy. In this way the three rioting Union regiments at the burning camp would be caught between Confederate forces coming from north and east, pushing the Federals south to the Belmont landing, where more of General Polk's arriving troops would be concentrating. The elder Louisianan marched his command of two regiments west and then south, with the Eleventh Louisiana in the lead followed by the Fifteenth Tennessee to the left rear.[15]

Remarkably, the only two regiments of the Confederate Reserve Brigade became lost and separated from each other in the thick woods of the Missouri interior; even more remarkably half of the companies of the Louisianans became separated from the other half! While Colonel Marks was trying to locate the various elements of his own regiment, acting Lieutenant Colonel Tyler's regiment, marching south, ran smack into the rear column of General McClernand's western-most regiment, the Thirty-First Illinois commanded by First Lieutenant Hibert A. Cunningham's brother-in-law, Colonel John A. Logan. Hibe had expected to meet Logan at Columbus, but certainly not in this manner.[16]

Unfortunately for Tyler, Logan's rear-guard companies were accompa-

Advance of the Fifteenth Tennessee at Belmont
1:15 PM, Thursday, November 7, 1861

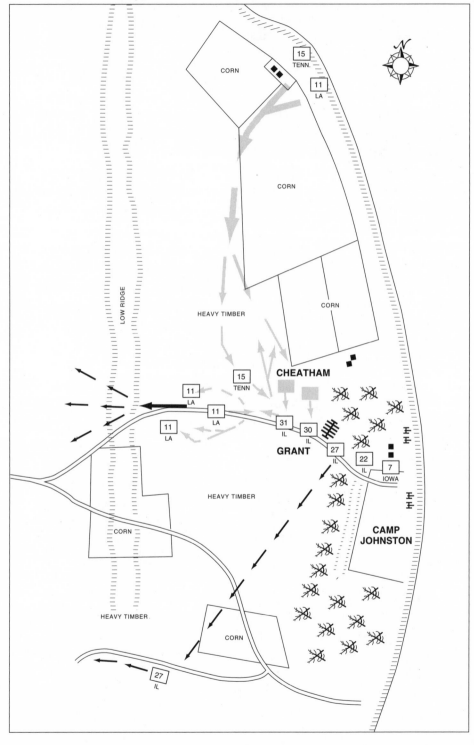

nied by two of the guns of Battery B, First Illinois Light Artillery Regiment, a predominantly Irish-Catholic unit out of Chicago sometimes referred to simply as the "Chicago Light Artillery (Irish)." A combination of Northern Illinois canister and Southern Illinois musketry stopped the Tennessean's accidental advance. In the first minutes of their first skirmishing action, six of Tyler's ten companies fled in panic to the rear, that is, to the northeast, through the forest to the river. It was not, to say the least, an auspicious beginning for the military history of the Fifteenth. With the Eleventh Louisiana still to the west and north and out of sight, the inexperienced acting lieutenant colonel was left to defend his improvised wooded position to the west and slightly north of the enemy with only about 220 men from four companies.[17]

The four officers and their commands were: Captain Matthew Dwyer and D Company (Major Hearn's original command from Madison County that, at first, had included Private Robert Charles Tyler), Captain W. B. Isler and E Company (the Madrid Bend Guards), Captain Nicholas Frech and I Company (the Washington Rifles, that is, the Germans from Shelby County), and Captain Thorndike Brooks and G Company (the Southern Illinois Company). At about 1:15 P.M. it became a case of brother-in-law versus brother-in-law with "Black Jack" Logan and his Southern Illinoisans firing away at Brooks, Cunningham, Hopper, Hays, Metcalf and their Southern Illinoisans. Logan and Brooks, along with the men of their units, were well aware that they were facing each other.[18]

In an act of considerable courage and perhaps considerable recklessness, Captain Isler requested and received Tyler's permission to lead a counterassault from northwest to southeast. The charge of the Madrid Bend Guards was cut to pieces by the Federal Southern Illinoisans and the Chicago Irishmen. Isler was mortally wounded and E Company suffered a number of casualties. Tyler, assisted by Dwyer, Frech, and Brooks, tenaciously held an impromptu defensive line in the woods near an opening off the road. Suddenly the men of G Company heard a roaring yell coming up from behind them to the right. When they turned an unforgettable image appeared from a spot of sunlight in the woods. Graybearded fifty-eight-year-old Colonel Sam Marks, on horseback waving his hat, was leading a bayonet charge.[19]

At the same time that companies of the Eleventh Louisiana struck companies of the Thirty-First Illinois, General Cheatham's Tennesseeans, Arkansans and Irishmen struck the back end of the Thirtieth Illinois of General McClernand's brigade and the front end of the Twenty-Second Illinois of Colonel Dougherty's brigade. As scattered elements of the Thirty-First and Thirtieth did an about-face and turned westward, they were accidentally ambushed by the companies of the Louisiana regiment that had been lost in the forest. The Federals were stunned.[20]

With his Seventh Iowa of Dougherty's brigade already badly banged up by the Memphis Irish Brigade (the Second and Twenty-First Tennessee) and with his Twenty-Seventh Illinois of McClernand's brigade off on a wild goose chase, General Grant had no choice but to withdraw his command from the field. The Illinoisan needed to get the main body of his five regiments back northwest to Hunter's Farm and away from Belmont, so that the men could fight another day. As Grant was retreating along the road and out of Camp Johnston, and as Cheatham was deploying his pursuit units from east to west at Camp Johnston, another of Polk's small brigades arrived at Belmont from Columbus along with the bishop-general himself. Colonel Preston Smith's command was formed from his own 154th Senior Tennessee Infantry Regiment (an old state militia unit with new recruits, many of whom were Irish-Americans and German-Americans) and the six companies of Lieutenant Colonel Andrew K. Blythe's First Mississippi Battalion Infantry.[21]

At 2:30 General Cheatham assigned Preston Smith's fresh troops to the front of his pursuing columns. Some of Colonel Logan's companies of the Thirty-First Illinois led the Federal withdrawal while some of his other companies served as rear guard for the retirement. When the men of the 154th Senior Tennessee took off after the rear companies of the Thirty-First Illinois, they were joined in flank by acting Lieutenant Colonel Tyler's remaining four companies of less than two-hundred men from the Fifteenth Tennessee, including the Southern Illinois Company, plus an equally small detachment of the equally exhausted Eleventh Louisiana. Shortly after 3:00 Logan decided that his best defense was an offense. For the purpose of clearing the enemy off his rear, he ordered a skirmish line assault south and east against the Confederate front. John A. Logan himself came riding out of the woods, appearing as he would many times in later battles, with his dark complexion and black mustache and mounted on a black horse waving his hat and leading his men on. It was at this time, during the last Union offensive movement, that Logan's horse was shot out from under him as the pistol at his side was shattered by an enemy ball.[22]

During the afternoon advance Second Lieutenant Harry Hopper of the Southern Illinois Company, out of shape and out of breath, was forced to fall behind. Also at this time Private Fred A. Jenkins, a Georgia-born Western Kentuckian, also of G Company, disappeared under mysterious circumstances. Given the position of Captain Brooks' men, well behind the Federal retreat, it would have been almost impossible for the missing enlisted man to have been captured. Much later it was learned that Jenkins was the first of two men out of the ninety-nine members of G company to formally betray his country by joining the Union Army.[23]

When Robert C. Tyler heard the firing to his front, he quickly swung his small skirmishing band to the left of Preston Smith's large Tennessee regiment as Andrew Blythe's Mississippians formed on the right. Thorndike Brooks' Southern Illinoisans, Western Kentuckians, and Middle Tennesseeans poured volley after volley into this very last reinforced Federal counterattack, inflicting several casualties. One of the Confederate combat officers to be noted for "coolness and determination" under fire was Brevet Second Lieutenant Harvey Hays of G Company and Williamson County, Illinois. Heavily outnumbered, John A. Logan, on a second black mount, withdrew his weary troops north along the road to Hunter's Farm, fighting a rear guard action all the way.[24]

By sunset the defeated Illinoisans and Iowans began boarding their transports for the demoralizing journey back up to Cairo. General Grant himself barely avoided capture. The men of the gallant four companies of the Fifteenth Tennessee desperately needed rest and relaxation. Better than forty years after the Battle of Belmont, Frank Metcalf fondly remembered that evening. With his shirt covered with sweat and blood, Harvey Hays "sat on a tree stump drinking from his flask with a grin on his face, having lived his dream of punishing the hated Yankee foe."[25]

Actually there wasn't all that much to celebrate on either side. Even if the partial Federal expedition was considered a mere reconnaissance-in-force, General Grant didn't learn anything he didn't already know about the solid strength of the Columbus garrison. General Polk, on the other hand, with an entire army corps at his disposal around Columbus, had taken all day to chase five enemy regiments away from Belmont, attaining a tactical victory that held no strategic gain.[26]

Out of about 2,500 men engaged the Federals suffered 95 killed, 306 wounded, and 205 captured or missing for a total of 606 losses or twenty-four percent of those engaged. Out of about 5,200 men engaged the Confederates suffered 105 killed, 419 wounded, and 117 captured or missing or twelve percent of those engaged. Out of slightly more than two-hundred men engaged the four companies of the Fifteenth Tennessee suffered ten killed, ten wounded, and one captured or missing (Jenkins) for a total of twenty-one losses or about ten percent of the engaged. Out of exactly forty-seven men engaged G Company suffered three wounded plus the traitor, Jenkins, for a total of four losses or eight and a half percent of the engaged. The three wounded men were: Corporal Samuel Cree of McCracken County, Kentucky; Private A. R. McKinelley of Williamson County, Illinois; and Private A. H. Morgan of Graves County, Kentucky, who was disabled for life.[27]

As the War Between the States entered its second year, the officers on both sides had a great deal of work to do. Near the top of the list was acting Lieutenant Colonel Robert Charles Tyler, whose duty it was to form all ten of his companies into one serviceable combat unit. Most frustrating of all was the fact that all four of Colonel Charles M. Carroll's English-speaking Memphis companies had bolted at Belmont. As it turned out in battle, the heart and soul of the regiment had been the Madison County men, the Lake County men, the Germans, and the Southern Illinois Company, not a comforting thought at that time. All six captains who had fled when the first shots were fired at them were consequently replaced by younger and more competent line officers from other commands. All six new captains had been lieutenants during the battle. Brigades at Columbus were then reorganized into larger and more practical units.[28]

Along with Colonel Knox Walker's Memphis Irishmen from the Second Tennessee, the Fifteenth Tennessee was added to Colonel Preston Smith's brigade, with Lieutenant Colonel Marcus J. Wright commanding the 154th Senior Tennessee. Lieutenant Colonel Andrew Blythe's battalion was reinforced by four independent Mississippi companies to form the Forty-Fourth Mississippi Infantry, giving Smith a fourth regiment. Two of these units were considered to be full regiments—the 154th Senior Tennessee and the Forty-Fourth Mississippi. The other two units were so undersized that they had to be considered mere skirmish line detachments—the Second and Fifteenth Tennessee. Colonels Smith, Walker, Wright, Blythe and Tyler worked together to get the brigade battle-ready. (Tyler's commission as a lieutenant colonel came through from Richmond on December 26, 1861.)[29]

In Middle Tennessee Confederate Fort Henry, on the Tennessee River, fell to U.S. Navy forces on February 6, 1862. General Gideon Pillow was then sent by General Sidney Johnston to Fort Donelson, on the Cumberland River, where the pompous Middle Tennessean promptly made another mess out of Southern fortunes in the West. Fort Donelson, where Colonel Logan fought with valor before being seriously wounded, surrendered to General U.S. Grant's Army and Navy forces on February 16, giving new meaning to the Illinois general's initials—"Unconditional Surrender." Pillow, on the other hand, would always be remembered as the general who left his own command behind prior to the surrender. As the result of these back-to-back Confederate disasters, General Leonidas Polk was trapped in the river system between Union commands from Southern Illinois down to West Tennessee, which meant that the city of Memphis would soon be a goner. Johnston ordered Polk to evacuate Columbus and all of Kentucky on February 20, as General Charles F. Smith's brigade was occupying the Middle Tennessee towns of Clarksville and Nashville. Moving slowly as usual, the bishop-general did not have all of his men out of the garrison until March 2. Colonel Preston Smith's brigade, along with other Columbus troops, was sent by rail down into West Tennessee through Union City and Jackson to the railroad town of Corinth, Mississippi just below the Tennessee border and a few miles southwest of the Tennessee River town of Pittsburg Landing, Tennessee near a Methodist meetinghouse known as the Shiloh Church.[30]

During the period of time from April of 1861 until April of 1862, not a single word appeared in any Southern Illinois newspaper about Thorndike Brooks or his compatriots from Williamson and Jackson Counties. Since there was no recognition, there was also no condemnation. This media silence was part of a small-scale cover-up to avoid embarrassment for Jack Logan. Even some of his closest supporters believed Logan to be guilty of encouraging Hibe Cunningham and the others to fight for the South. Interestingly enough, no Illinois Unionist *ever* criticized the thirty-four Illinois Confederates of Company G for doing what they did. After recovering from his Fort Donelson wound, former Congressman John A. Logan was given command first of a brigade and then of a division. On March 13, 1863, he was promoted from brigadier general to major general of volunteers. He then commanded the XV Corps, Army of the Tennessee, and at the July 22, 1864, Battle of Atlanta, he brilliantly took command of that army. Major General John A. Logan became, in fact, the Union counterpart of Lieutenant General Nathan Bedford Forrest, that is, the very best *civilian* high-ranking general in the army. Following the war Logan conveniently changed party affiliation from Democrat to Republican and was elected as a United States Senator from Illinois. In 1884 the Southern Illinoisan was the unsuccessful Republican nominee for Vice President of the United States. The debate continues to this very day as to whether or not the man accidentally or deliberately misled many of his Democratic congressional constituents in Egypt about his anti-abolitionist leanings toward secession. Jack Logan denied the accusations until the day he died. Mary Cunningham Logan, a loving wife and mother, supported the version of her brother, Hibert, over the version of her husband. The ultimate truth must lie in the eye of each and every historical beholder.[31]

Chapter Four
Twelve Minutes of Fame at Shiloh

Captain Thorndike Brooks and G Company of the Fifteenth Tennessee pulled into the depot at Corinth on March 9, 1862, with sixty officers and men present for duty, including Brooks himself. Brigadier General Bushrod Rust Johnson then replaced Colonel Preston Smith as brigade commander, with Smith returning to the command of the 154th Senior Tennessee. Johnson, a scholarly Ohio-born Quaker from Nashville, had led a two-brigade division with distinction at Fort Donelson. The day after the Fifteenth Tennessee arrived in the state of Mississippi, New Madrid and Island Number Ten fell, leaving the Federals in control of the Mississippi River all the way down to Memphis. With Western Kentucky completely gone and with West Tennessee nearly gone, General Sidney Johnston was gathering an army together on the Tennessee-Mississippi border for the purpose of preventing a Union penetration into the deep South.[1]

Bushrod Johnson's Brigade at Shiloh

2nd Tenn. .... Colonel J. Knox Walker
15th Tenn. .... Lieutenant Colonel Robert C. Tyler
154th Senior Tenn. .... Colonel Preston Smith
44th Miss. .... Lieutenant Colonel Andrew K. Blythe
Polk's Tennessee Battery .... Captain Marshall T. Polk

By the end of March, Johnston had assembled 40,335 officers and men, including the sixty members of the Southern Illinois Company, forming them into four division-sized corps. The corps were commanded by Major Generals Braxton Bragg (six brigades), Leonidas Polk (four brigades), William J. Hardee (three brigades), and Brigadier General John C. Breckinridge (three brigades). Two of Polk's four brigades formed a division commanded by Frank Cheatham; one of Cheatham's two brigades was commanded by Bushrod R. Johnson; one of Johnson's four regiments was commanded by Robert C. Tyler; and one of Tyler's ten companies was commanded by Thorndike Brooks.[2]

Major General Henry Halleck, who had replaced Frémont as commander of all Union forces in the main Western theatre, encouraged by the February successes at Forts Henry and Donelson, was inspired to do something. With a heavy nudge from President Abraham Lincoln, Halleck was determined to push Johnston further into Mississippi and Alabama with the hopes of crippling the enemy army. Responsibility for a two-pronged assault was given to Major General U. S. Grant's Army of the Tennessee (six full divisions of eighteen brigades of 42,682 effectives) and to Major General Don Carlos Buell's Army of the Ohio (four divisions of about 20,000 effectives).[3]

On St. Patrick's Day the lead elements of Grant's army sailed south up the Tennessee River to the town of Savannah, Tennessee, the landing immediately above Pittsburg. In the next few days these troops steamed south to establish a large Federal camp at Pittsburg Landing, Tennessee, placing themselves in a position that was only twenty-five miles northeast of Johnston's Confederate Army of the Mississippi at Corinth, Mississippi. While Grant was concentrating his forces along the Tennessee from Savannah to Pittsburg Landing, the elusive, slow-moving Carlos Buell was on the march from Bowling Green, Kentucky, through Nashville into Middle Tennessee swinging west with the intent of hooking up with Grant for the strike against Johnston.[4]

General Sidney Johnston's plan of battle was the only possible one that could save the Western Confederacy. The Texan determined to march from Mississippi back up into Tennessee and launch a surprise attack with his full force against Grant's southernmost position before the Illinoisan could be reinforced by Buell. The Southerners, including Brooks' company of Tyler's regiment of Johnson's brigade of Cheatham's division of Polk's corps of Johnston's army, moved out of Corinth undetected on the morning of Friday, April 4, and cautiously crossed the state border. By the following day five Union divisions were already posted at Pittsburg Landing, with the other division still up at Savannah with General Grant himself, giving Johnston a slight numerical advantage in the coming battle. Commanding Grant's Fifth Division at Pittsburg Landing was Major General William Tecumseh Sherman, the Ohioan who was back in action after having been relieved the previous year for emotional problems. Later that evening Sherman wired Grant that all was quiet on the Western front. Just before dawn on Sunday morning, April 6, 1862, the men of G Company, Fifteenth Tennessee crept through the woods along the Corinth Road toward the enemy camp. Straight ahead the darkness was broken by the isolated glow of a few early breakfast fires. Forty-four of the Southern Illinois Company's remaining sixty officers and men had come up from Corinth. A realization struck Sergeant Frank Metcalf and Private Spince Blankenship at the same time. The Yankees had been caught completely off guard.[5]

At the beginning of the surprise attack, General Johnston, coming up the road with his troops, deployed an assault wedge that consisted of General Hardee's corps up front, to be followed by General Bragg's corps, with General Polk's corps forming to the rear of Bragg, and with General Breckinridge's corps in reserve. General Bushrod Johnson's brigade of General Cheatham's division of Polk's corps marched to the rear of Colonel Robert M. Russell's brigade, which formed the left wing of Brigadier General Charles Clark's division, also of Polk's corps. Clark's other brigade was commanded by Brigadier General Alexander Peter Stewart, another Tennessean who, without orders, snatched up Colonel Sam Marks' Eleventh Louisiana of Russell's brigade and half of Knox Walker's ten companies of the Second Tennessee of Johnson's brigade to supplement his command. Polk then instructed Cheatham to move Johnson to the left and rear of Russell, a movement that not only made Johnson the left flank of Polk's corps, but also the left flank of Johnston's entire army. In his order of battle Johnson fanned out to the extreme left of the Confederate advancement, deploying a line that left to right consisted of half the Second Tennessee, the Fifteenth Tennessee, Captain Marshall T. Polk's Battery (Company G, Artillery Corps of Tennessee), the Forty-Fourth Mississippi, and the 154th Senior Tennessee. Colonels Walker and Tyler were to the far left of the army with Colonels Blythe and Preston Smith to the right of the brigade's artillery. Johnson assigned Tyler's regiment as infantry support for Marsh Polk's guns, which isolated Walker's small band of Irishmen on the far left. To the woods in front of him Captain Brooks

Major General Bushrod Rust Johnson in 1863.

could hear the rising crescendo of battle as Hardee's troops slammed into the line of the surprised Federals.[6]

The largest of Grant's six divisions was Sherman's (four brigades), which had more men than two of Johnston's four corps. The Ohioan's big unit had been awarded the position of honor, farthest from the Pittsburg Landing. Three miles out, on the Corinth Road, Sherman's divisional headquarters tent was pitched alongside the small log building identified as Shiloh Church. Two of the general's brigades were in line to the west, extending over to Owl Creek, which flowed into Snake Creek where it turned northwest, a mile from the Tennessee, leaving Owl Creek to protect the Union right flank south of that area. These two all-Ohio brigades, each of three regiments, were commanded by Colonels Ralph P. Buckland and Jesse Hildebrand. The other two brigades of the Fifth Division were posted on the opposite far sides of the Ohioans. In this way the Federals had unwisely trapped themselves between Owl and Snake Creeks with their backs to the Tennessee River.[7]

However, in Sherman's mind that morning, as in Grant's, the main concern was getting ready to move out to Corinth as soon as Buell arrived from Nashville. The roaring of Confederate cannon at 4:30 A.M. changed all of that. Sherman, an excitable person who was completely calm in battle, reacted quickly and ordered the six regiments of Buckland and Hildebrand to their rifle pits on high ground. Grant had just begun to eat his breakfast at Savannah when he heard the blast of guns at Pittsburg Landing.[8]

The Shiloh Church sector of the Pittsburg Landing battlefield was the Union right, Confederate left. The task of General Sherman's two middle brigades was to block the Corinth Road. The small Methodist meetinghouse sat just to the south of that road. To the immediate north of the road was Colonel Buckland's brigade (Sherman's center). Deployed from south to north, left to right, were Captain Samuel E. Barrett's four-gun battery (Battery B) of the First Illinois Light Artillery Regiment, the Irishmen from Chicago who had fought at Belmont, then the Seventieth, Forty-Eighth, and Seventy-Second Ohio Infantry. This brigade held down the best position of any of the blue-clad units on the field. It occupied a valley whose slope was steep and bushy with a bend, giving the Seventieth Ohio an enfilading fire (cross fire).[9]

To the immediate south of the road was Colonel Hildebrand's brigade (Sherman's left). Deployed from south to north, left to right, were the Fifty-Third Ohio, Captain Allen C. Waterhouse's four-gun battery (E Battery) of the First Illinois Light Artillery Regiment, also out of Chicago, the Fifty-Seventh Ohio, and the Seventy-seventh Ohio. Between the Seventy-Seventh of Hildebrand and the Seventieth of Buckland was Shiloh Church.[10]

As Captain Thorndike Brooks marched his men north to the sound of battle, it became obvious to the Southern Illinoisan that the surprise element had been lost to the Boys in Gray early in the action because of problems with troop movements, communications, and command structure. General A. P. Stewart had already acted independently of Generals Polk, Clark, Cheatham, and Bushrod Johnson. There were too many chiefs and not enough Indians. The rapid intermingling of Confederate units hurt cohesion and grew more chaotic as the fighting intensified. At 7:30 two of General Hardee's brigades, commanded by a pair of young general officers from Arkansas, came off the Corinth Road and attacked General Sherman's defensive line at Shiloh. The four regiments of Brigadier General Thomas C. Hindman advanced against Hildebrand's position on Hardee's right, while Irish-born Brigadier General Patrick R. Cleburne's six regiments advanced against Buckland's position on Hardee's left. The two Chicago Batteries of Waterhouse and Barrett inflicted heavy casualties on the gray-clad infantry. The Confederate Irishman, a tremendous fighter, assaulted twice but was battered back with a loss of a third of his large brigade.[11]

General Bragg, coming up next in line, moved his corps too slowly to support Hardee's corps. Bragg, a weak field commander, had the deadly habit of fighting his troops piecemeal. As Cleburne was slammed back the second time, Bragg rode to the rear toward the nearest arriving brigade of Polk's corps with orders to renew the attack against Buckland. Strictly by accident this unit was Johnson's brigade of Cheatham's division. But before Johnson could move up in support of Hardee's corps or Bragg's corps, Bragg detached the two large regiments of the brigade on the right—the Forty-Fourth Mississippi and the 154th Senior Tennessee—and sent these troops further to the right under Colonel Preston Smith for the purpose of supporting the Confederate forces moving against

Hildebrand and Waterhouse. With Smith commanding a two-regiment "demi-brigade," Lieutenant Colonel Marcus J. Wright again commanded the 154th Senior Tennessee as he had at Belmont. General Cheatham witnessed the action between Colonels Smith and Hildebrand. As the fighting heated up, Cheatham, acting as his own staff officer, started moving some of Smith's companies around on the battlefield, a highly unusual duty for a division commander.[12]

Bushrod Johnson was faced with going up against the strongest Union position in the Shiloh sector (Buckland and Barrett) with a demi-brigade consisting of Captain Marshall T. Polk's six-gun Tennessee battery, Colonel Knox Walker's unhappy five companies of the isolated Second Tennessee, and Lieutenant Colonel Robert C. Tyler's small and suspect Fifteenth Tennessee, including the forty-four officers and men of the Southern Illinois Company. Very few American generals have ever been presented with a more difficult task with so small a command. Worse yet, the Nashville brigadier had been given no instructions by Bragg, while Polk was nowhere to be found and Cheatham was off directing traffic with Preston Smith. Amazingly, General Polk, the corps commander, soon joined General Cheatham, performing the duties of another staff officer by directing the flow of the various companies of the two regiments of Lieutenant Colonels Blythe and Wright! Again it was too many chiefs and not enough Indians.[13]

By 8:30, under a heavy cross fire of musketry from Colonel Joseph R. Cockerill's Seventieth Ohio Infantry, General Johnson had managed to align Marsh Polk's guns in a clearing of the woods off the road across the field from Irish-Chicagoan Sam Barrett's four guns, with Tyler's 450 men in support to the front of the battery, and with Walker's loudly cursing 150 Confederate Irishmen to the rear of the battery. M. Polk's assignment was to silence Barrett and his Union Irishmen. The plan for the infantry was designed to have Walker eventually move up and join Tyler, but it never happened. Johnson described the opening action in his own words:

> *In the position taken by the left wing the Fifteenth Regiment Tennessee Volunteers occupied the ground in front, and the Second Regiment Tennessee Volunteers was posted in the rear of Polk's battery. The Fifteenth then advanced some 200 yards under heavy fire.*[14]

Position of the Fifteenth Tennessee at Shiloh
8:30 AM, Sunday, April 6, 1862

Tyler's front column of skirmishers, the Swiss Rifles, followed by the Washington Rifles, moved cautiously through the woods to a position that was a mere one-hundred paces in front of the most formidable enemy position on Sherman's front, the Seventieth Ohio and Barrett's Irish battery. Cockerill's musketry and Barrett's canister swept the ranks of the Memphis Germans, causing a momentary wavering of Tyler's front line. The lieutenant colonel had to draw his revolver to restore order. It was not, however, the Germans of the Fifteenth who broke and ran; it was the remaining Irishmen of Knox Walker's five companies of the Second Tennessee who then fled in panic. The Memphis Irish-Americans, who had performed well at Belmont, resented being separated from their comrades and being isolated from the other units at the same time. The breakup of the Irish regiment proved to be a disaster for Johnson, who rode to the rear in a vain effort to stem the tide, leaving Tyler alone in command at the forward position to confront the enfilading fire of Cockerill and Barrett.[15]

It was shortly after the general left that the lieutenant colonel was seriously wounded, as his horse was shot out from under him. Dr. John M. Wall of G Company, who had been serving as an aide to Tyler, rode to his commander's rescue, took him to the rear, and gave him the medical assistance that saved his life. At that moment Major John F. Hearn was serving as an aide to General Cheatham over on General Johnson's right opposite Colonel Hildebrand's front. There was considerable confusion in the ranks of the Fifteenth as to which captain was senior and supposed to take command. While Tyler's regiment, still alone on Johnson's left flank, continued to suffer heavy casualties, Marsh Polk had one of his legs shattered by shrapnel, causing even more confusion among the remaining captains. After Tyler and M. T. Polk fell, Bushrod Johnson returned to the front and bestowed regimental command to the officer who had been holding the infantry together—Captain Thorndike Brooks of Williamson County, Illinois, and the Southern Illinois Company.[16]

Colonel Joseph Cockerill checked his pocket-watch and later testified that Brooks and his men held the line of the Confederate detachment for twelve minutes under a murderous crossfire. As the Nashville Quaker rode to the rear a second time in a futile effort to bring Walker's Irishmen up, he was seriously wounded. As Johnson was carried off, he gave Wall a message for Brooks. The Southern Illinoisan was instructed to retire in an orderly fashion, while saving the six guns at all costs. The brigade commander was justifiably concerned that a confused withdrawal would cause the cannon to be abandoned.[17]

Barrett's Irish gunners from Chicago, supported by the riflemen of the Seventieth Ohio, continued to blaze away at Polk's gunners, supported by the infantrymen of the Fifteenth Tennessee and a very small remnant of the Irish Second Tennessee. Using the two German companies of his front column as rear guards for the retreating Tennessee artillerymen, Captain Brooks ordered rotating bursts of musketry to be fired. Sergeant Samuel H. Graham, the Minnesota Confederate of G Company, joined the Rebel Germans and fired round after round from his musket at the position held by Cockerill's Ohioans. Also in the Southern Illinois Company, Second Lieutenant Harry Hopper, who had sore feet, proved to be of little use, while Brevet Second Lieutenant Harvey Hays, who was drunk, did little more than yell a litany of curses at the blue-clads. First Lieutenant Hibe Cunningham got into a dispute with an officer of the Irish regiment and was, consequently, not much more of a factor than Hopper or Hays. Even worse, seven of the enlisted men of G Company joined the disgruntled Memphis Irishmen and ran to the rear in panic.[18]

The seven cowards were Privates J. M. Cooper of Knox County, Tennessee; Henry Gifford of Williamson County, Illinois; S. T. Jones of Graves County, Kentucky; A. J. Lowe of Williamson County, Illinois; J. F. Parkhill of McCracken County, Kentucky; J. P. Price of Knox County, Tennessee; and J. M. Summerville of Graves County, Kentucky.[19]

Other enlisted men of the Southern Illinois Company performed extremely well. During the early stages of the retirement, Private W. W. Haywood, the fifty-nine-year-old Nashville, Davidson County Tennessee, drummer was disabled for life by fragments from one of Captain Barrett's exploding shells that lodged in his legs, thighs, and back. Private Ronald M. Randall of Williamson County, Illinois, temporarily saved his wounded brother, Private Calvin Randall, by removing him from the battlefield, even though he was slightly wounded himself. Calvin died six weeks later. At about the same time that Haywood and Calvin Randall fell, the color-bearer of the Fifteenth Tennessee (a soldier from Madison County, Tennessee, whose name was not given) was cut down by one of

Colonel Cockerill's riflemen, leaving the survivors of the color-guard in a state of confusion, their facial expressions dazed.[20]

Sergeant Frank Metcalf of Jackson County, Illinois, organized an improvised flag detachment consisting of Sergeant P. Timothy Corder, Jr., Corporal P. Timothy Corder, Sr., Private Spince Blankenship, Private J. T. Roland, Private M. V. Williams, and himself. When Metcalf grabbed onto the flag pole, the other five rallied the remnant of the color-guard. As the elder Tim Corder was wounded, his higher-ranking son helped him remain on his feet. Unfortunately, due to a lack of medical assistance from Dr. Wall, who was treating General Johnson, the wound proved to be mortal and Tim, Sr., died exactly one week later. Roland suffered multiple wounds and, in spite of being helped off the field by the reliable young Williams, died seven weeks later. Despite the carnage, the mission of Brooks and Metcalf was accomplished. The standard and four of the six pieces of artillery were saved. Metcalf, the two Corders, Blankenship, Roland, and Williams were the men from Jackson County who had joined up with Thorndike Brooks at the Delaware Crossing of the Saline River. So this is how is came to pass that all six Carbondale Confederates served with great distinction at Shiloh. (Captain Marsh Polk himself was less fortunate. He was captured by the Federals whose medical team saved his life by amputating his leg. The battery reported four killed, eighteen wounded, and two missing, including Polk, out of the 102 men engaged. Two of the six guns were destroyed by Barrett's Battery, and thirty out of eighty-one horses were killed. Polk's Battery was disbanded at Corinth a mere few weeks after the Battle of Shiloh.)[21]

At about 9:20 A.M., after some fifty minutes of deadly combat on the left flank of Bushrod Johnson's brigade, other Southern units moved up, as the gallant soldiers of the Fifteenth fell back to lick their wounds. Captain Brooks' twelve-minute stand had prevented the far Confederate left from collapsing in front of Sherman's division. General Sherman himself reported that "Buckland's brigade was the only one with me that retained its organization." Buckland's brigade most especially included the commands of Joseph Cockerill and Samuel Barrett. The Fifteenth, under the worst of circumstances, was bested by the best. Johnson stated firmly that his efforts against Colonel Ralph Buckland's three heavily dug-in regiments would have been much more successful had the situation been different:

From unavoidable necessity, my labors during the heat of the action were mainly confined to the extreme left of the brigade. I have to regret that, from orders apparently given to the subordinates of my command, I was prevented from bringing the whole brigade together handsomely into action. To this object all my efforts had been zealously and carefully directed. Had I accomplished my purpose, I am convinced I would now have to report much more satisfactory results.

(It was General Cheatham, not General Johnson, who identified Generals Bragg and Stewart as the culprits who had separated Johnson's four regiments.)[22] Tyler's regiment had 473 officers and men engaged in the Battle of Shiloh (or Pittsburg Landing), of whom 189 were killed, wounded, captured, or missing for a staggering 40 percent of the total. The Fifteenth Tennessee was decimated. Of the sixty officers and men of G Company who were present for duty at Corinth, forty-four were brought up to Pittsburg Landing but seven of them, as mentioned, refused to advance at Shiloh Church. Of the thirty-seven men engaged in battle eight were killed or mortally wounded, six were wounded (five of whom were disabled), and six were captured for total losses of twenty out of thirty-seven, that is, a horrific 54 percent of those engaged. Company G was decimated, the dreams of a "First Illinois Confederate" regiment long gone.[23]

The eight members of the Southern Illinois Company who gave their lives for the Southern cause at Shiloh were: Corporal P. Timothy Corder, Sr., of Jackson County, Illinois; Private C. F. Carmon of Graves County, Kentucky; Private W. J. Davis of Williamson County, Illinois; Private J. T. Gunn of Graves County, Kentucky; Private James Mowlen of Rutherford County, Tennessee; Private G. L. Patterson of Williamson County, Illinois; Private Calvin Randall of Williamson County, Illinois; and Private J. T. Roland of Jackson County, Illinois.[24]

Some fifteen or twenty minutes after the shattered Fifteenth Tennessee left the field, Sherman's defensive line protecting the Corinth Road began to crumble under the weight of the Confederate numbers. The first of the six Ohio regiments to break was the Fifty-Third of Hildebrand's brigade; the very last Union front line regiment to fall back from Shiloh Church was the Seventieth of Buckland's brigade which, along with

Barrett's Irish-Chicago battery, had done nearly all the damage to Tyler's command. The men of the Fifteenth Tennessee, including G Company, had held their own against the best of the best. Late in the morning Grant arrived to supervise his divisions.[25]

In another sector, dubbed the Hornet's Nest, south of the landing and east of the church, Sidney Johnston launched a massive assault against the Federal Sixth Division, commanded by Brigadier General B. M. Prentiss, the former colonel of the Tenth Illinois, who almost exactly a year earlier had sent three companies from Cairo up to quell the "uprising" at Carbondale. The Confederate army commander was wounded in the leg at 2:30 P.M. and bled to death near the Peach Orchard, south of the Hornet's Nest. The slain Johnston was replaced by his second-in-command, General P. G. T. Beauregard, the fiercely independent and obstinate little Creole from Louisiana. After an extraordinarily heroic stand, Prentiss and 2,200 of his men surrendered at 5:30. By this time the Northerners, still trapped between the two creeks, had been pushed back east almost to the Pittsburg Landing of the Tennessee River, having wedged themselves into a box with water on three sides of the box and with the entire Confederate Army poised to strike the only open end of the box. The Southerners, with an aggressive evening pursuit, could have bagged the whole lot of them and changed forever the course of the war in the West. Beauregard had been against the idea of a surprise attack from the beginning of the plan. With faulty scouting reports at his disposal, he called off operations at 6:00 P.M., incorrectly believing that Buell could not come down in time to prevent the destruction of Grant's army in the morning. As it turns out the early defensive deployment of the six Ohio regiments and the two Chicago batteries from Sherman's middle brigades had bought Grant just enough time to survive the day.[26]

The bloodied Fifteenth Tennessee was kept in reserve during the second day of battle. At 7:30 A.M. on Monday, April 7, Major General U. S. Grant counterassaulted General Beauregard with Major General Lewis Wallace's Third Division of the Army of the Tennessee on his left and with Major General Don Carlos Buell's Army of the Ohio on his right. The Confederates were pushed back west to Shiloh Church, where another huge slugfest took place for most of the day. In the end Union numerical strength won out. With no reinforcements coming up from the Confed-

erate Army of the West (Trans-Mississippi theatre of operations) under
Major General Earl Van Dorn, Beauregard withdrew to Corinth. The
Southern surprise attack on April 6 was one of the best conceived and
worse executed offensive movements in American military history. Grant,
bailed out by Sherman, had won a tremendously important victory. The
Confederate defeat on April 7, 1862, cost the South its best chance to
prevail in the Western theatre. Casualties for the two days were astound-
ing. The Federals lost 13,047 men killed, wounded, captured or missing,
including sixty-three blue-clads of the Seventieth Ohio. The Confederates lost 10,694 men killed, wounded, captured, or missing, including
those 189 gray-clads of the Fifteenth Tennessee, twenty of whom were of
G Company. Shiloh was the first of the huge, bloody battles of the War
Between the States. The American people, North and South, were shocked
by the realization that the conflict would be a long and desperate one.[27]

Although the Southerners did not evacuate Corinth until May 29–30,
the Fifteenth Tennessee, along with General Bushrod Johnson's other three
regiments, fell back to Tupelo, the Mississippi railroad town below
Corinth, where the banged-up command was reorganized on May 11.
Not surprisingly, Colonel Charles M. Carroll was not re-elected. The
highly respected Major John F. Hearn was detailed as a staff officer by
General Frank Cheatham. Lieutenant Colonel Robert C. Tyler was elected
as regimental colonel. Based on his cool and determined performance at
Shiloh, Captain Thorndike Brooks was elected the lieutenant colonel.
Versatile First Lieutenant John M. Wall was elected the major. The election of the three regimental staff officers caused Brooks to pass over the
rank of major and Wall, who as surgeon was a brevet captain, to pass over
the permanent rank of captain. Brooks, in fact, forever became the highest ranking Illinois resident in Confederate service, while Wall rose from
noncombat to combat status. Since Tyler was still down with his wound,
the top two field officers of the Fifteenth were both men from G Company. As a result of this, Thorndike Brooks became unique in one other
respect. He was the only Illinois resident to ever command a Confederate regiment. Another Southern Illinoisan, Sergeant Frank Metcalf, was
given the high-risk honor of becoming regimental color-bearer. The reason for the success of G Company men at the re-election was obvious.
The Southern Illinois Company, no longer a source of camp jokes, had

left Shiloh with a solid combat reputation. At the time of the regimental reorganization some of the wounded were reporting back for duty. With 323 officers and men present at Tupelo, Lieutenant Colonel Brooks transported the Fifteenth Tennessee back up to Corinth, where the original ten companies were reorganized on May 15, prior to the evacuation.[28]

Two companies, both destroyed at Shiloh, were dissolved. The remnant of A Company was attached to E Company and the remnant of K Company, the Swiss Rifles, was attached to I Company, the Washington Rifles, in an obvious effort to keep the hard-fighting "Germans" (foreign-born Europeans) together. Brooks was left with a command of eight companies, each of about forty men. Company G had three officers and thirty-four enlisted men present for duty. When Thorndike Brooks moved up the ladder to the regimental staff, his top three company subordinates, all formerly members of the Twelve Apostles, followed him. Hibert A. Cunningham was elected as captain of the company with Henry C. Hopper as his first lieutenant and with Harvey L. Hays as his second lieutenant. Because the same officers were retained, this small unit continued to be referred to as the Southern Illinois Company. Samuel H. Graham, the Minnesotan who was handy with a musket, was elected as the company's sergeant major, the top enlisted man.[29]

Good buddies Harry and Harvey didn't last very long. On exactly the same day that he was elected to the permanent rank of second lieutenant Hays got involved in a series of drunken disturbances with other officers and men and, as a result, was cashiered from the army by no-nonsense Colonel Tyler, still recovering from his Shiloh wound. In June of that same year of 1862, Hopper went on sick leave and never returned, leaving Cunningham as the only commissioned officer of G Company. To fill the leadership gap, a special election was called for the position of second lieutenant. Because of the dwindling size of the company, the position of first lieutenant was left vacant. Bryant W. Hudgens, age twenty-one, a well respected soldier from Cheatham County, Tennessee, was elected to replace both Hopper and Hays, becoming the sixth and last commissioned officer of G Company of the Fifteenth Tennessee Infantry. Hudgens would prove to be a more valuable combat officer than Hopper and Hays put together.[30]

According to highest rank achieved, the six officers to come out of the

Southern Illinois Company were Lieutenant Colonel Thorndike Brooks of Williamson County, Illinois; Major John M. Wall of Graves County, Kentucky; Captain Hibert A. Cunningham of Williamson County, Illinois; First Lieutenant Henry C. Hopper of Williamson County, Illinois; Second Lieutenant Harvey L. Hays of Williamson County, Illinois; and Second Lieutenant Bryant W. Hudgens of Cheatham County, Tennessee. Of interest is the fact that all six officers had achieved their highest rank during the middle of the war's second year and were never promoted after that.[31]

After the regimental and company reorganizations, the Fifteenth was sent back down to Tupelo on June 6, where they went into bivouac while awaiting three-year re-enlistments. On July 20 of that sizzling Mississippi summer of 1862, fifteen of the enlisted men of G Company, including all six who had been captured and exchanged at Shiloh, failed to re-enlist and were formally discharged from the army. Seven others were transferred or deserted. Two were discharged because they were under age. Privates B. L. Walston and M. V. Williams, already ten-month veterans, were both seventeen. Private Williams of Jackson County, Illinois, had helped Sergeant Robert Kelly to escape at Linn's Hotel and had helped Sergeant Frank Metcalf to rally the regimental color-guard at Shiloh.[32]

In August Lieutenant Colonel Thorndike Brooks' regiment was transferred to General Braxton Bragg's expanded command. What followed was a long journey by rail and by foot down to Mobile, Alabama, and then all the way back up into Tennessee. When the Boys in Gray crossed the Kentucky border in September, Brooks counted 274 regimental officers and men present for duty. For practical deployment purposes, the Southern Illinoisan divided his undersized regiment into a pair of company-sized battalions. Companies B, C, D, and E were consolidated under the command of Major John M. Wall, while Companies F, G, H, and I were consolidated under the command of Captain Hibert A. Cunningham. These were field consolidations and individual company muster rolls continued to be maintained. The remnant of G Company, a mere squadron consisting of exactly one officer and ten enlisted men, was commanded by Second Lieutenant Bryant W. Hudgens. Officers Brooks, Wall, Cunningham, and Hudgens were all members of the original Southern Illinois Company.[33]

The remaining ten G Company enlisted men were: Sergeant Major Samuel H. Graham of Minnesota; Sergeant Frank Metcalf of Jackson County, Illinois; Private Jeremiah Ables of McCracken County, Kentucky; Private Spince Blankenship of Jackson County, Illinois; Private A. J. Dillard of Graves County, Kentucky; Private John Finnegan of Williamson County, Illinois; Private Edward Gomand of Giles County, Tennessee; Private Asa G. Morris of Davidson County, Tennessee; Private Robert Mullens of McCracken County, Kentucky; and Private Frank Ogle of Humphreys County, Tennessee.[34]

By September of 1861, ninety-nine men had registered for G Company of the Fifteenth Tennessee Infantry. By September of 1862, fourteen of the ninety-nine were still present and accounted for. Five of the fourteen were from Southern Illinois—two officers (Brooks and Cunningham) and three enlisted men (Metcalf, Blankenship, Finnegan). This small band of Southern patriots had one more assignment ahead of them before disappearing into the obscurity of American history.[35]

Chapter Five
Glory at Gibson's Farm
Perryville

President Abraham Lincoln clearly stated the importance of his native state of Kentucky to the Union: "I hope to have God on my side, but I must have Kentucky. I think to lose Kentucky is nearly the same as to lose the whole game." The President felt that without the presence of Rebel troops, Kentuckians would rally to the Union banner. Lincoln was right. When General Polk evacuated Columbus in March of 1862, Federal Kentuckians seized control of the state. Four months later President Jefferson Davis, also a native Kentuckian, determined to pull the Bluegrass state back down into the Southern fold. The President felt that without the presence of Yankee troops Kentuckians would rally to the Confederate banner. Davis was wrong. When Braxton Bragg, replacing the slain Sidney Johnston, finally got around to invading Kentucky in the fall, the people of Kentucky resisted.[1]

With the Southerners in full retreat following Shiloh, Abraham Lincoln had control not only of all Kentucky, but also of all West and Middle Tennessee. Naturally he turned his attention in the Western theatre to pro-Union East Tennessee, ironically the last Confederate military foothold in the Volunteer State. The President strongly reinforced General Buell's Army of the Ohio and gave the Ohioan instructions to drive all remaining enemy forces out of East Tennessee. By mid-July of 1862 Buell was commanding a force of ten divisions of about 69,000 effectives strung out along the Tennessee Railroad from Corinth to Chattanooga.[2]

The highly organized General Bragg, with a much smaller command than Buell's, produced a well conceived plan of action against the uninspiring Union general. The North Carolinian initiated the first Confederate counterassault in the West. Bragg planned to invade Federally-occupied Kentucky, causing Buell to abandon East Tennessee and pursue the invading Southern army up into Bluegrass country. The plan worked. Carlos Buell followed Braxton Bragg with the same type of troop movements that characterized his military career—very slow. Unfortunately for Jefferson Davis, Bragg planned a great deal better than he executed. The resulting Kentucky Campaign would prove to be a meaningless series of baffling troop movements, with both sides avoiding the other like the typhoid.[3]

General Bushrod Johnson's badly battered Shiloh brigade was broken up, and the Nashville Quaker was given a fresh command. On August 18, 1862, Lieutenant Colonel Thorndike Brooks and the men of the Fifteenth Tennessee Infantry were attached to the all-Tennessee brigade of Brigadier General Daniel Smith Donelson, a grizzled sixty-year-old Tennessee veteran of the Mexican War, whose name had been bestowed on the already fallen Cumberland River fort. Colonel Robert Charles Tyler, still officially the commanding officer of the Fifteenth, continued to recuperate from his Shiloh wounds by serving as a staff officer for General Frank Cheatham's division. The other four Tennessee regiments of Donelson's brigade were the Eighth, Sixteenth, Thirty-Eighth, and Fifty-First. This was one of the four brigades that formed Cheatham's division, each brigade of five regiments, eighteen of the twenty regiments from Tennessee, including the Fifteenth. Actually there were only three other divisions in General Bragg's entire Army of the Mississippi. General Polk's corps ("the right wing") consisted of the divisions of Cheatham and Brigadier General Jones Withers. General Hardee's corps ("the left wing") consisted of the divisions of Major General Simon B. Buckner and Brigadier General J. Patton Anderson.[4]

Daniel Donelson's Brigade at Perryville

8th Tenn. .... Colonel William L. Moore
15th Tenn. .... Lt. Colonel Thorndike Brooks
16th Tenn. .... Colonel John Savage
38th Tenn. .... Colonel John Carter
51st Tenn. .... Colonel John Chester
Carnes' Tennessee Battery .... Captain William W. Carnes

During that same summer of 1862, the Confederate Department of

East Tennessee was commanded by Major General Edmund Kirby Smith. This command was a detached army corps of four divisions, two large (four brigades each) and two small (two brigades each). The Richmond, Virginia, War Department kept Kirby Smith's two full divisions at Chattanooga for the purpose of holding the vital East Tennessee town. His two small divisions under Brigadier Generals Patrick Cleburne and Thomas Churchill had been detached from Bragg's army. This latter force of four brigades of about 7,000 effectives was referred to during the Kentucky Campaign as the "Army of Kentucky," which was in reality a single full division. All together Bragg's army of invasion had four divisions and one detachment of twenty brigades of about 34,000 effectives, including the fourteen officers and men of the Southern Illinois Company, to go up against Buell's ten divisions of thirty brigades of some 69,000 effectives, giving the Ohioan a numerical advantage of slightly better than two to one.[5]

On August 30, Kirby Smith's reinforced detachment defeated Major General William "Bull" Nelson's division, detached from Buell's army, at the Kentucky town of Richmond. The Southern invaders were not warmly welcomed by most of Kentucky's citizens and Bragg picked up only a few recruits for his army. Carlos Buell kept the division of Brigadier General George Morgan behind in southeastern Kentucky and sent his other nine divisions, including the remnant of Nelson's, marching along the Louisville and Nashville line to the city of Louisville on the Ohio River opposite the Indiana border, which meant that by mid-September the pursuers were geographically well ahead of the pursued.[6]

While Buell was supplying his army at Louisville, Bragg marched his four divisions, along with Kirby Smith's detachment, up to the town of Frankfort, east of Louisville. It was here that the Southern commander made the symbolic and meaningless gesture of "inaugurating" Richard Hawes as the Confederate governor of Kentucky. When Buell's scouts informed him of the enemy presence in Frankfort, he sent the division of Brigadier General Joshua Sill over east to divert Bragg from the Union main thrust. Hawes' "acceptance speech" was interrupted by Sill's artillery.[7]

Leaving Kirby Smith's four brigades behind to block Sill's four brigades in front of Frankfort, Bragg proceeded to do what he usually did in most

Major General Benjamin Franklin Cheatham in 1864.

situations. He retreated. His destination was the town of Lexington below Frankfort. For reasons that are not obvious, General Bragg believed
that General Sill's division at Frankfort was really the main body of General Buell's army. Consequently he left General Kirby Smith's command
at Frankfort and deployed General Jones Withers' command at Lexington convinced that "Buell" would have to go through Smith and Withers
to get at him. In reality the main elements of eight Federal divisions were
still up near Louisville.[8]

That summer had been exceptionally hot and dry and both armies badly
needed to water men and animals. The Confederate commanding general felt secure in sending his other three divisions (Cheatham, Anderson, Buckner) down to the villages of Bardstown and Harrodsburg to find
water in the many creeks around that area. Cheatham's division, at that
moment of three brigades, including Donelson's with the Fifteenth Tennessee and the Southern Illinois Company, traveled further south than
the other two gray-clad divisions and camped at the hamlet of Perryville
below Harrodsburg.[9]

On October 3, with President Lincoln expressing considerable impa-
tience with his snaillike western commander, General Buell moved out
from Louisville and marched southeast for the dual purpose of finding
water and doing battle with Bragg. In spite of the fact that the Federal
columns churned up a cloud of dust that could be seen for many miles in
all directions, General Bragg clung to the belief that the enemy army was
directly north at Frankfort, being hedged in by Kirby Smith and Jones
Withers. On the evening of October 7, the vanguard of the three blue-
clad divisions of Major General Charles C. Gilbert's Third Corps arrived
in Perryville to discover that much of the water had already been con-
sumed by the three brigades of General Frank Cheatham, including D. S.
Donelson's brigade with the Fifteenth Tennessee and the Southern Illinois Company. Behind Gilbert were the five available divisions from Buell's
other two corps under Major Generals Thomas L. Crittenden and
Alexander McCook.[10]

General Braxton Bragg was exceedingly pleased to hear reports about
the enemy "watering party" down in Perryville. With "Buell" back up in
Frankfort, he eagerly ordered his divisions of Anderson and Buckner down
to join Cheatham for an early morning attack that would allow him to

concentrate his forces against the meager Union detachment. The Confederate general could foresee breaking off the enemy command piece by piece. A decisive action against the Federal watering party at Perryville would be exactly the right place to begin. As it turned out the watering party was eighty per cent of the Army of the Ohio, some 55,000 officers and men.[11]

On the morning of October 8, 1862, General Don Carlos Buell established his headquarters just south of Harrodsburg and about two and a half miles north of Perryville. With his advance units tired and thirsty Buell called off the planned operations for that day. Because he postponed his scheduled attack against enemy forces south of him until October 9, the Northern commander gave his subordinates deployment instructions that called for them to hold their fire while avoiding combat for October 8. These orders would prove to be a considerable problem in the light of the Confederate assault on that very day. Remarkably Generals Buell and Gilbert would sit in their tents most of October 8 not knowing that the Battle of Perryville was being fought. Given the hundreds of rounds of artillery that were fired that day, both the top-ranking Yankee generals must have been deaf as well as dumb.[12]

At 8:00 A.M. on that same Wednesday of October 8, as General Buell was ordering his breakfast, a lonely General Cheatham, facing the main body of the enemy army alone with his division posted along the banks of the Chaplin River at Perryville, was joined by Generals Polk, Hardee, Anderson, Buckner, Bushrod Johnson, A. P. Stewart, George Maney, and Donelson. It was still too many chiefs and not enough Indians. Since all of these Southern gentlemen were of sound minds, they quickly formed the opinion that the Northern force opposite them was somewhat larger than a watering party. Given the fact that only two of Hardee's brigades had, at that point, come down to support Polk's three brigades under Cheatham the generals felt compelled to abandon Bragg's plan of battle, with the intent of digging in on defense by constructing temporary breastworks on the east bank of the Chaplin River, thereby inviting Carlos Buell to attack from west to east across the river. General Leonidas Polk, as the army's second-in-command, took full responsibility for the decision with support from the others.[13]

At 10:00 General Braxton Bragg himself arrived on the scene in an especially foul mood, even for him. Publicly reprimanding the bishop-general for not following instructions, the usually unaggressive command-ing general again ordered an assault from east to west, contending that the blue-clad troops were merely a "reconnaissance-in-force." At this point, not only was Bragg's wisdom in question but so also was his sanity. So this is how it came to pass that eight Federal divisions of about 55,000 men were attacked by five Confederate brigades of about 9,500 men, while the Union commander sat in his tent two miles away poring over his maps planning his troop movements for the next day, and while the Confeder-ate commander insisted that the Union commander was thirty-five miles away awaiting the return of his watering party.[14]

Bragg moved the three brigades with Cheatham at Perryville, includ-ing Donelson's, from the Confederate left to right, deploying the main body of the division to the left of Colonel John A. Wharton's cavalry bri-gade, which was posted on the extreme right end of the line, putting the men of the Fifteenth Tennessee at the opposite flank of the army than the one that had been assigned at Shiloh. It took two hours for Lieutenant Colonel Thorndike Brooks to prepare for a confrontation with the en-emy "reconnaissance-in-force" by marching his men from Walker's Bend westward over a bridge of the Chaplin River and then south to a set of bluffs, a perfect position to observe the extreme Union left a mile further to the south. At about 12:00 P.M. Brooks discovered that General Bragg, as army commander, had done to Donelson's brigade exactly what he had done, as corps commander, to Bushrod Johnson's brigade at Shiloh. He had divided it. Earlier that morning the commanding general had detached Battery D of the First Tennessee Light Artillery Regiment under Captain William Carnes from Donelson and sent it left to the Confederate cen-ter, supported by the Eighth and Fifty-First Tennessee regiments, also of Donelson's brigade, creating a demi-brigade commanded by Colonel Robert C. Tyler, leaving old General D. S. Donelson with only three small regiments of about one-thousand effectives—the Fifteenth, Sixteenth, and Thirty-Eighth Tennessee, that is a demi-brigade the size of a single full regiment with no artillery cover. (Twenty-three of Captain Carnes' gun-ners at Perryville had served with Captain Marsh T. Polk at Shiloh.)[15]

By 1:00 the troops on both sides assumed the same essential positions on the line that they would hold for the next six hours. On the Federal left west of the river, about three miles distant directly opposite General Cheatham's three brigades with Brooks and the Fifteenth Tennessee, were the available five brigades (without General Sill's four brigades) of General McCook's corps. In the center was a division, three brigades, of General Gilbert's corps commanded by a new young brigadier—Philip Henry Sheridan, who would become the United States Army's best known Irish-American soldier. Opposite "Little Phil" was a single brigade of three Mississippi regiments from General Patton Anderson's division. On the Federal right a single brigade of General Crittenden's corps faced a single brigade of General Buckner's division under General Bushrod Johnson.[16]

Shortly before 1:30 Bragg ordered Polk to open the attack on the Confederate right/Union left as soon as all of Cheatham's men finished crossing the Chaplin River to the west bank. Polk attached Wharton's three cavalry regiments, which could fight mounted or dismounted, to Cheatham's two-and-a-half infantry brigades. From their right to left Polk and Cheatham deployed the brigades of John Wharton, George Maney, D. S. Donelson (three regiments only), and A. P. Stewart. At 2:00 the men of Cheatham's reinforced command advanced three-quarters of a mile through an open field which sloped towards Doctor's Creek, one of the many small bodies of water which flowed through that area. Once on the western side of the creek, Generals Polk and Cheatham began to direct the gray-clad units. Wharton and Maney (the eight regiments on the Rebel far-right flank) charged through a heavily wooded area toward the position held by the two startled brigades (seven regiments) of Brigadier General James S. Jackson's division of McCook's corps. To the left of Maney, Cheatham advanced his other eight Tennessee regiments, with Donelson's three units, including the Fifteenth, to the front of the movement and with Stewart's five units to the right and rear, a deployment that put Donelson on the left end of Cheatham's right wing. Defending themselves against the eight regiments of Stewart and Donelson would be elements of the three surprised brigades (fourteen regiments) of Brigadier General L. H. Rousseau's division of McCook's corps.[17]

The Sixteenth Tennessee Infantry, commanded by Colonel John Savage, was a veteran regiment from the Cheat Mountain campaign on the Eastern front. Savage's officers and men made up about half (five-hundred) of Donelson's October 8 detachment. The Thirty-Eighth Tennessee Infantry, like the Fifteenth, had been in the Western theatre from the beginning. Whereas the Sixteenth consisted primarily of men from Warren County, the Thirty-Eighth, like the Fifteenth, consisted primarily of men from Shelby County. Colonel John Carter, the commanding officer of the Thirty-Eighth regiment, had about the same number of effectives as Brooks, that is, some 250 officers and men. General Donelson, on the left of General Cheatham's front line, deployed Colonel Savage on the right, Lieutenant Colonel Brooks on the left, and Colonel Carter to the rear behind Brooks, a deployment that made the Fifteenth Tennessee the extreme left flank regiment of Cheatham's right flank division.[18]

The Southern Illinois Confederate deployed Major John M. Wall's battalion of the Fifteenth on his left, with Captain Hibert A. Cunningham's battalion on his right, a move that posted Wall's four companies on the far left end of Polk, Cheatham, Donelson, and Brooks. Second Lieutenant Bryant W. Hudgens' G Company squadron of eight enlisted men was with Cunningham's command. Sergeant Frank Metcalf was at the front of Major Wall's command, with the regimental colors of the Fifteenth Tennessee Infantry. Private Spince Blankenship was a member of that color-guard.[19]

To the south in front of a bluff, Brooks, Wall, Cunningham, Hudgens, Metcalf, Blankenship, and the eight men of Hudgens' squadron could see an open pasture about 260 yards wide and some five-hundred yards long, bordered on both sides by woods. Enemy infantrymen, supported by six guns, appeared behind a rail fence at the far end of the field. The two blue-clad units were Lieutenant Colonel Oscar F. Moore's Thirty-Third Ohio Infantry of Colonel Leonard A. Harris' brigade of General Rousseau's division and Captain Samuel J. Harris' Nineteenth Battery of the Indiana Light Artillery Regiment of Colonel George Webster's brigade of General J. S. Jackson's division.[20]

At 2:15 Cheatham moved Donelson's three regiments onto a knoll in the woods to the right of the field. Cheatham's instructions to Donelson were to silence Samuel Harris' battery, while driving Leonard Harris' lead companies away from the fence. Initially this was to be bayonet charge. Shortly before 2:30 Donelson's demi-brigade emerged from the trees, faced right, and marched along the open pasture toward the fence, spearheaded by the skirmishers of the Sixteenth Tennessee. Brooks was to the left and

Assault of the Fifteenth Tennessee at Perryville
4:30 PM, Wednesday, October 8, 1862

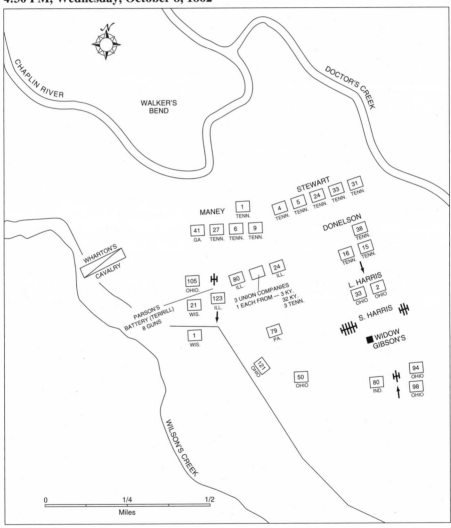

rear of Savage, with Carter to the left and rear of Brooks.[21]

Instead of the expected confrontation with the infantry and artillery of L. A. Harris and S. J. Harris, the startled Tennesseeans were stopped by fire from other Yankees concealed further south in those same woods to the right of the field. It was the canister of Captain Charles Parsons' six-gun battery, supported by musketry from detached companies of Brigadier General William R. Terrill's brigade of three regiments, Jackson's division. John Savage's regiment and Hibe Cunningham's four right flank companies of Thorndike Brooks' regiment were heavily fired on. John Carter's regiment was not yet engaged. One of Charles Parsons' first blasts inflicted multiple wounds on Frank Metcalf, as Spince Blankenship took possession of the flag pole.[22]

Wisely taking the battlefield initiative, General D. S. Donelson quickly altered General Cheatham's plan by fast-stepping his assault wedge widely to the left away from the menacing elements of General Terrill's brigade, advancing his columns in a southwest direction into the woods to the left of the field opposite Captain Parsons' gunners. Between 2:45 and 3:00 Donelson's men, using the same deployment as before, emerged from the wooded area that bordered the left side of the field, turned left, and charged directly down the pasture from north to south. With bayonets extended, the veterans of the Sixteenth Tennessee led by Colonel Savage on horseback ran right up to the rail fence, screaming the Rebel yell, and assailed the Thirty-Third Ohio of the mounted Lieutenant Colonel Moore, who was still supported by four of the guns of Captain Samuel Harris' Hoosiers. At this point it was discovered that Captain Cunningham's battalion of the Fifteenth, including Second Lieutenant Hudgens' Southern Illinois squadron, had already been knocked out of the fight by General Terrill's riflemen and Captain Parsons' gun crew, as Hudgens and Sergeant Major Samuel H. Graham, the Minnesota Confederate, successfully rallied a small remnant of Cunningham's command with the whereabouts of the captain himself unknown. Lieutenant Colonel Brooks came up on General Donelson's left with Major Wall's battalion in an effort to assist the beleaguered Colonel Savage, as Private Blankenship advanced with the colors of a dwindling regiment.[23]

The same problem persisted. Thanks to General Bragg's juggling act, the Tennesseeans of Donelson's demi-brigade had no artillery cover. By

3:15 the effective fire power of Samuel Harris' four remaining guns of the Nineteenth Battery, Indiana Light Artillery, had forced the Tennessee Boys in Gray to fall back into the woods to the left of the field. This temporary lull in the action gave Colonel Leonard Harris the opportunity to move another regiment from his brigade up on the right of the hard-pressed Thirty-Third Ohio. This unit, accompanied by Samuel Harris' other two guns, was Leonard Harris' own original regiment—the Second Ohio Infantry, then commanded by Lieutenant Colonel John Kell.[24]

While the fighting raged on all three sectors of the Perryville battlefield, Generals Buell and Gilbert continued to be blissfully ignorant. When General McCook finally arrived at Perryville, he was informed by Generals Crittenden and Rousseau that Generals Jackson and Terrill had already been killed. In fact the only Union commander to enjoy much success was General Sheridan at the center. The aggressive and ambitious young West Pointer had slammed his three brigades into the middle position of the gray-clads, pushing piecemeal troops of Generals Simon Buckner and Patton Anderson some two-hundred yards to the east. An angry Sheridan would later be ordered by Buell to fall back to his original position. As McCook was being briefed by Rousseau between 3:00 and 3:30, he found Buell's instructions in his pocket. They were simple to understand: *Do not engage.* Fortunately for the Union cause, the three simple words had been disregarded by all the Boys in Blue for several hours, ever since General Bragg had fired his first artillery salvo against the watering party.[25]

At the same time that General Alex McCook was trying to organize his scattered corps units into a defensive stand, a badly bleeding Sergeant Frank Metcalf was being carried to the rear by the stretcher bearers of General Frank Cheatham's staff. The members of the Confederate medical team believed that the Carbondale color-bearer was about to die. They were wrong. Metcalf would live two days shy of another fifty-five years. While the wounded sergeant was being attended to, General Donelson was giving his subordinates the same order of battle. Colonel Savage would assault on Donelson's right against the left flank of Colonel Leonard Harris' brigade (Lieutenant Colonel Moore and the Thirty-Third Ohio), while Lieutenant Colonel Brooks on the left front, supported by Colonel Carter to the rear, assaulted the right flank of Harris' brigade (Lieutenant Colonel Kell and the Second Ohio). The intent was also the same. Drive the enemy infantry to the south so that the guns of Captain Samuel Harris' battery could be overrun, silenced, and captured.[26]

The men of the Second Ohio were posted in the Widow Gibson's cornfield at the right end of Leonard Harris line; behind Kell were two of the guns of Samuel Harris' Nineteenth Battery of the Indiana Light Artillery. These infantrymen and gunners blocked the approach of Dr. Wall's battalion of the Fifteenth Tennessee. At the left end of Leonard Harris' Federal line the Thirty-Third Ohio still held the rail fence; behind Moore were the other four guns of Samuel Harris' crew. At 3:45 Donelson moved forward again with the same negative results. On the elderly Tennessean's right, opposite Moore, the hard-fighting John Savage was wounded and his regiment was forced back, again with heavy losses. On Donelson's left, opposite Kell, Wall's battalion of Brooks' regiment was quickly dispersed, because the remnant of the missing Cunningham's disorganized battalion could not be moved up in time to assist Wall, in spite of the strong efforts of Hudgens and Graham. It was all over in fifteen minutes or less. Tennessee drummers pounded out the beat of a second retreat. D. S. Donelson, however, stubbornly clung to his only plan of battle—attack the enemy wherever he stands. The hard-nosed Tennessee veteran ordered a third assault for 4:30. Only this time Thorndike Brooks and his small unit would be used as a decoy. Following the second retirement Hibe Cunningham reappeared.[27]

Brooks, Wall, Cunningham, Hudgens, Graham, and Blankenship of the Southern Illinois Company, along with the remaining men of the Fifteenth Tennessee (probably no more than 150 of them), again advanced their skirmishers through Mrs. Gibson's corn as the musketry of the Second Ohio (probably no more than two-hundred of them) and the canister of the Nineteenth Indiana Battery (two guns) whistled by them. Out of the woods to the left of the cornfield sprang Colonel John Carter and the rested men of the Thirty-Eighth Tennessee (still about 250 of them). With a numerical advantage of about two to one, Carter and Brooks struck Kell simultaneously. It was at this point that the assault-wedge of the Confederate demi-brigade of three regiments penetrated the line of the Union demi-brigade of two regiments. On the other end of the Donelson-Leonard Harris line, the gallant Colonel Savage and the Sixteenth Tennessee (down to about three-hundred men) for the third time charged the rail fence and participated in hand-to-hand combat with the gallant Lieutenant Colonel Moore and the Thirty-Third Ohio (also down to about three-hundred men). Unfortunately for the blue-clads the other three regiments of Harris' brigade had become engaged with elements of General A. P. Stewart's brigade. Consequently, the Union brigade commander could not bring up any support units to confront General Donelson. Colonel Leonard Harris described the early stages of the enemy breakthrough.

> *I retired to the woods in the rear of the cornfield where I met the Thirty-Third Ohio who had just replenished their cartridges. At this time the Second Ohio was warmly engaged with the enemy, stubbornly falling back, and husbanding their ammunition, which was nearly exhausted.*[28]

Shortly after this the two guns of the Hoosier battery with Lieutenant Colonel John Kell were captured by Captain Hibe Cunningham and the men of his greatly reduced command, who had finally come up from the rear. Private Spince Blankenship, suffering minor wounds, and the color-guard of the Fifteenth Tennessee, continued to advance with Major Wall's men. By 5:00 the Thirty-Third Ohio, like the Second Ohio earlier, was experiencing an ammunition shortage. In spite of being wounded a second time, the valiant Colonel John Savage surged forward one more time, causing Lieutenant Colonel Oscar Moore to yield the rail fence, as Colonel Leonard Harris' thin line began to collapse. General D. S. Donelson, with three regiments of about one-thousand men and no artillery against two regiments and one six-gun battery of about eight-hundred men, had won the fight for Gibson's Farm after three full frontal assaults and at a heavy human cost. The coordinated third attack of Colonels Savage, Brooks, and Carter had pushed Colonels Harris, Moore, and Kell one-hundred yards to the south, but Donelson had no rested reserve units with which to actively pursue the defeated foe. General Alex McCook prevented any possibility of a rout on that sector of the Perryville battlefield when he reinforced Leonard Harris' two weary front line regiments with two other nearby regiments, the Twenty-Fourth Illinois Infantry of Colonel John C. Starkweather's brigade of General L. H. Rousseau's division, and the Eighteenth Indiana Infantry of Colonel George Webster's brigade of the late General J. S. Jackson's division.[29]

By 6:00 most of the fighting on General Frank Cheatham's right flank (north end) of the battlefield had temporarily stopped for the reloading of cartridge boxes. Both sides redeployed as best they could with Cheatham's four brigades, including Donelson's, continuing to face McCook's five brigades, including Leonard Harris' four-regiment detachment. Brooks, with Wall's company-sized command, was assigned to hold up the left rear of Donelson's line to reinforce Carter's command, with Savage's depleted command still up on the right. Cunningham's less than company-sized command, including Hudgens' Southern Illinois squadron, was posted in reserve on the eastern crest of the hill on which the Widow Gibson's barn stood. During this latest lull in the storm, Cheatham moved Tyler's demi-brigade to the front of Donelson's demi-brigade, reuniting the entire command of five regiments and one battery under the aging Tennessee general. The newly deployed front line of Donelson's brigade, commanded by Tyler, consisted of the Eighth and Fifty-First Tennessee, fresh companies of the Thirty-Eighth Tennessee, and Carnes' battery. The exhausted Donelson commanded his own thin second line of a few hundred troops, that is, the remnant of the Sixteenth Tennessee, the much smaller remnant of Wall's half of the Fifteenth Tennessee, and the banged-up companies of the Thirty-Eighth Tennessee. At 7:00 Cheatham led a renewed thrust against McCook's impromptu defenses, using the infantry brigades of Maney and A. P. Stewart. D. S. Donelson ordered R. C. Tyler to advance against the reinforced position of Leonard Harris. When Donelson and Tyler were in turn reinforced by the Twenty-Fourth and Thirty-First Tennessee regiments of Stewart's brigade, Colonel Leonard Harris' Northerners were pushed another one-hundred yards to the south, further away from the Chaplin River. Captain Samuel Harris' remaining four guns were then captured by Tyler. Crusty old Donelson, like so many other Southern officers, became "an eyewitness to his [Tyler's] courage, managing his men with the greatest skill and efficiency."[30]

General Buell finally found out about the size of the battle to the south of him late that afternoon. Amazingly he refused to alter his plan of attack for the morning of Thursday, October 9. As a result he withdrew the only Federal troops to have made any real progress—General Sheridan's. By 8:00 the autumn sky had turned dark. General Bragg ordered a halt to hostilities. General Polk ordered the colonel of the Eighty-Seventh

Indiana Infantry to cease firing, only to discover that he had been trying to command enemy troops. The bishop-general slipped away in the darkness.[31]

By the time that Buell got around to his scheduled movement in the morning, Bragg had already characteristically withdrawn. The Battle of Perryville, an insane confrontation that neither side had intended to fight that consisted of about a two-hundred-yard Confederate advance, had been a useless bloodbath. Only nine out of thirty Union brigades and only five of twenty Confederate brigades were fully engaged. Out of 36, 940 officers and men the Northerners lost 4,211 killed, wounded, captured, or missing for a total of eleven percent of those engaged. Out of 15,990 officers and men the Southerners lost 3,396 for twenty-one percent. In the Fifteenth Tennessee thirty-four men were killed or disabled. The number of wounded, captured, or missing was never recorded by the army. However, an examination of the muster rolls following the battle indicates that the regiment lost about forty percent of its combatants.[32]

Out of the fourteen officers and men engaged, G Company lost one man killed and three wounded. Giving his life for the Southern cause at Perryville was Private A. J. Dillard of Graves County, Kentucky. The three wounded were Sergeant Frank Metcalf, Private Spince Blankenship, and Private John Finnegan, all Southern Illinoisans, the first two of Jackson County and the color-guard, the last of Williamson County. Metcalf, who had been wounded in several places by canister, was later transferred to the Invalid Corps. Finnegan, who was also captured, was eventually sent to Camp Butler where he was exchanged by the Union Army and then discharged because of his wounds by the Confederate Army. Blankenship, who was wounded for the first of three times, recovered fully and continued to serve with great distinction in the Fifteenth Tennessee.[33]

General Braxton Bragg's retreat from Kentucky to Tennessee came a mere two weeks after General Robert E. Lee's retreat from Maryland to Virginia following the bloody Battle of Sharpsburg (Antietam Creek). Southern morale also went south. President Abraham Lincoln replaced Major General Don Carlos Buell and Army of the Ohio with Major General William S. Rosecrans and the Army of the Cumberland, which was essentially the same command reinforced by other Western units. On December 16, 1862, Colonel Robert C. Tyler was appointed by Bragg as

Provost Marshall of the Army of Tennessee, leaving Lieutenant Colonel Thorndike Brooks as commanding officer of the Fifteenth Tennessee for another four months. At Murfreesboro, Tennessee, (Battle of First Murfreesboro, or Stone's River) on the last day of 1862 and the first two days of 1863, General Bragg fought General Rosecrans to a standstill, but again retreated. In spite of the fact that the Fifteenth was detached from General Donelson's brigade for guard duty and not engaged at Murfreesboro, Brooks and Major John M. Wall were both wounded by enemy sharpshooters, an extremely unlucky circumstance. By April 1, 1863 Tyler, no longer with any special assignments, was back in command of the Fifteenth with Brooks and Wall, recovered from their wounds, serving again as his top subordinates. Company G was dissolved. The Fifteenth Tennessee Infantry would be reorganized one more time.[34]

Postscript

On June 6, 1863 the Fifteenth Tennessee was reduced to two companies (A and B) of 162 officers and men present for duty. Second Lieutenant Bryant W. Hudgens' tiny G Company squadron was attached to the new A Company. On that same day another small Tennessee infantry regiment, the Thirty-Seventh, was reduced to two companies of 177 officers and men. The two units were combined as the Fifteenth/Thirty-Seventh Tennessee Consolidated Infantry Regiment. Colonel Robert C. Tyler of the Fifteenth, as senior in rank, was the commanding officer. The officers of the Thirty-Seventh, from both Middle and East Tennessee, did not like the arrangement that gave leadership to a stranger. In order to pacify them, this was considered a field consolidation with muster rolls maintained separately for the two original outfits. The senior lieutenant colonel of the consolidated regiment was Robert Dudley Fraser of the Thirty-Seventh, a graduate of the Kentucky Military Institute. Still recuperating from his Murfreesboro wound, Lieutenant Colonel Thorndike Brooks was briefly listed as commanding officer of the Fifteenth. But within a month sickness, complicated by the wound, forced him to return to sick leave until February of 1864, leaving Major John M. Wall as ranking officer of the Fifteenth and as third ranking officer of the Fifteenth/Thirty-Seventh.[1]

On November 12, 1863, during the Chattanooga campaign, a series of cause-effect promotions took place. When Major General Simon B. Buckner was transferred from General Braxton Bragg's army to General Joseph E. Johnston's army, Major General John C. Breckinridge was promoted from division to corps command. As the result of this, Brigadier General William B. Bate of Tennessee was promoted from brigade to division command, Tyler was promoted from regimental to brigade command, and Fraser was promoted from commanding officer of the Thirty-Seventh Tennessee to commanding officer of the Fifteenth/Thirty-Seventh

Tennessee Consolidated with Wall as his second-in-command. When Dudley Fraser went down with a wound at the November 25, 1863, Battle of Missionary Ridge, Wall took command of the regiment. In spite of the fact that Colonel Tyler was seriously wounded, General Bate held fast on the center crest of the ridge longer than any other Confederate commander, thanks in large measure to the efforts of Major Wall and the other regimental commanders of Tyler's brigade. Missionary Ridge proved to be Bate's first and last outstanding performance as a division commander. Colonel Thomas Benton Smith of Tennessee became brigade commander, as the recuperating Tyler was deservedly given the rank of brigadier general. The command situation changed again in February 1864, when both Fraser and Brooks returned to active duty. When Colonel R. Dudley Fraser took permanent command of the consolidated regiment, Lieutenant Colonel Thorndike Brooks and Major John M. Wall again became the top two officers of the Fifteenth. Major Rufus M. Tankesley then became the lieutenant colonel of the Thirty-Seventh. It should be noted that unlike Wall, Brooks commanded only the Fifteenth, never the Fifteenth/Thirty-Seventh, not even briefly.[2]

During the embarrassing Tullahoma campaign (June to August, 1863), General Bragg retreated the Army of Tennessee completely out of the Volunteer State without engaging the enemy in a major battle. Eleven of the ninety-nine original members of G company were accounted for on the muster roll of A Company of the Fifteenth, including officers Brooks, Wall, Cunningham and Hudgens. Private Jeremiah Ables of McCracken County, Kentucky, was captured on May 23, 1863. As a prisoner of war at Louisville, he was exchanged within a few days. Declared unfit by the Medical Review Board, he was discharged from the army on June 24.[3]

The uneven Confederate military career of Captain Hibert A. Cunningham soon drew to a thoroughly non-glorious conclusion. In May, 1863, Hibe requested and received a furlough, July 1 to September 1. He never returned to the army. From September 15, 1863, until February 1, 1864, he was listed as AWOL. In February of 1864 he was officially branded as a deserter. In fact, it was worse than that. Cunningham was the second and last member of the Southern Illinois Company and the only Southern Illinoisan to go over to the other side. In the fall of 1863 he walked into his brother-in-law's tent and was given the commission as a captain in the Union Army, serving as an aide to Major General John A. Logan.[4]

Private Asa G. Morris of Davidson County, Tennessee, was engaged in a skirmish at Hoover's Gap, Tennessee (near Tullahoma), before being critically wounded in north Georgia at Reed's Bridge during the Chickamauga campaign, September 18, 1863. Morris, who barely avoided death, was confined to two military hospitals—in Atlanta and in Savannah—for a period of one full year. In October 1864 he was assigned to the Invalid Corps. Private Frank Ogle of Humphreys County, Tennessee was captured during the Atlanta campaign at the June 27, 1864, Battle of Kennesaw Mountain. Sent to Camp Morton, Indiana, he was released at the end of the war.[5]

Major John M. Wall, the splendid soldier-surgeon from Graves County, Kentucky fought with distinction at the Battles of Chickamauga and Missionary Ridge. In the latter engagement Wall's Fifteenth/Thirty-Seventh Tennessee made a strong stand on the crest along with the Tenth and Thirtieth Tennessee regiments, also of Tyler's brigade of Bate's division. At the July 22, 1864, Battle of Atlanta the young officer was mortally wounded. Left on the battlefield, he bled to death two days later, a few hundred yards away from the tent of Union Captain Hibert A. Cunningham. As a result of the doctor's death, his descendants—potentially bright, energetic Americans—would never be born. But this was also the case with thousands of other fallen Civil War soldiers.[6]

Private Edward Gomand of Giles County, Tennessee participated in the battles of Hoover's Gap, Chickamauga, and Missionary Ridge. Wounded and captured on August 31, 1864, at Jonesboro, Georgia during the Atlanta campaign, he was exchanged on September 19 and then released to the Invalid Corps.[7]

One of the most unlikely heroes of the South, Sergeant Major Samuel H. Graham, was engaged at Hoover's Gap, Chickamauga, Missionary Ridge, and all of the battles of the Atlanta campaign. During this time his skill with a musket caught the attention of his division commander, Major General William B. Bate. By special orders from Bate himself, the Minnesota Confederate was placed on extra duty as a sharpshooter during General John Bell Hood's ill-fated counteroffensive into Tennessee in the fall of 1864. Severely wounded in the neck by musketry fire at the

Battle of Franklin on November 30, Graham never fully recovered from his wounds, which were complicated by disease. Giving his life for his adopted country, the Minnesotan died January 12, 1865, and is buried at the McGavock Confederate Cemetery at Franklin.[8]

Another Northern hero of the South was Indiana-born Private Spince Blankenship of Jackson County, Illinois, a versatile soldier who had served with the color-guard at Shiloh and Perryville. The Carbondale resident was the only member of the Southern Illinois Company to be wounded in three separate battles—Perryville, Chickamauga, and Jonesboro. He was hospitalized all three times before being released to the Invalid Corps at Richmond, Virginia on February 15, 1865.[9]

When Hood marched his ragtag remnant of the Army of Tennessee to the south of Nashville in December of 1864, only three of the ninety-nine members of G Company were still present for duty. They were: Lieutenant Colonel Thorndike Brooks of Williamson County, Illinois (who served on Colonel Dudley Fraser's staff), Second Lieutenant Bryant W. Hudgens of Cheatham County, Tennessee (who was nearly blind), and the obscure Private Robert Mullens of McCracken County, Kentucky. All three made it all the way through to the very end, surrendering with General Joe Johnston at Greensboro, North Carolina, April 26, 1865. Of the thirty-four Southern Illinoisans who served in G Company only two are known for sure to have lived in the state of Illinois after the war—Cunningham and Kelly.[10]

Seven days after General Robert E. Lee surrendered the Army of Northern Virginia and ten days before Johnston surrendered the Army of Tennessee, a small skirmish took place at the Georgia hamlet of West Point. Brigadier General Robert Charles Tyler, commanding a meager garrison force, was killed instantly by a single shot from a Federal cavalryman. After the fort surrendered, the Confederates were allowed to bury their commander with full military honors. No relative ever came forward to claim the sword of the former private of D Company, Fifteenth Tennessee Infantry.[11]

Epilogue

In late March of 1908 an old man with a gray mustache and a limp, attired in his Sunday best, walked into the Nashville office of the *Confederate Veteran Magazine*. He was Frank Metcalf, age seventy-one, a gentleman farmer from the town of Mayfield in Graves County, Western Kentucky. The former sergeant of G Company, Fifteenth Tennessee Infantry, was warmly greeted by the diminutive editor of the popular magazine, another old sergeant, a compatriot from the Army of Tennessee. Sumner A. Cunningham (certainly no relation to Hibe) was a veteran of B company, Forty-First Tennessee Infantry, an outfit known as the "Richmond Gentrys" out of Bedford County, Tennessee. One of his most harrowing experiences of the war had been the Battle of Franklin, where S. A. Cunningham had been an eyewitness to the death of Brigadier General Otho F. Strahl, another Tennessean. Sergeant Metcalf of the Southern Illinois Company gave his article to Sergeant Cunningham of the Richmond Gentrys and then posed for the photographer. *The Illinois Confederate Company* appeared in the May issue. Not a single word on the subject would be published for another fifty-two years.[1]

Frank Metcalf, the Carbondale Confederate, died in his Kentucky home on October 6, 1917, two days shy of fifty-five years after he had suffered serious wounds defending the colors at Perryville. He was eighty-one years old.[2]

The only member of G Company known to have lived beyond Metcalf was Private Calvin Henderson Ferrell of Dyer County, Tennessee, the son of Irish immigrants who had fought under Brooks' command at Belmont and Shiloh. A Stewart County resident in 1861, he enjoyed a most successful postwar career. A merchant, gentleman farmer and businessman, Ferrell organized the Merchants State Bank at Humboldt, Tennessee (Dyer County) in 1887 and was elected as president that same year. Thirty-five years later in 1922, at the age of eighty-four, he still held the same position at the same bank.[3]

Appendix A

Individual Sketches and Compiled Military Service Records, G Company, Fifteenth Tennessee Infantry

Since next to nothing has ever been written about the men of G Company except for the one article and two letters of Sergeant Frank Metcalf, this book would not have been possible without the individual service records from the Tennessee State Library and Archives (TSLA), Nashville. In some instances these records provide virtually no personal information about particular veterans. In other instances, the information is somewhat interesting but useless. In still other instances these records provide the best available primary source materials. To these Tennessee state records the author has added bits and pieces form the National Archives and Records Administration (NARA) in Washington, D.C., regarding notes from the original muster rolls, identification cards, and army inspection reports. Illinois, Kentucky, and Tennessee census records were needed to identify most but not all of the birthplaces. Statistical accounts from the United States census of 1860 were also examined.

The recording of human history requires a compilation of events from the past and a consistent interpretation of those events. For this reason the author includes some editorial comments about some of the men within the body of the records, all of which are logical deductions based on facts. All care has been taken to avoid exaggeration. For example, Private Spince Blankenship, a Southern Indiana-born Southern Illinois resident who was wounded in action during three different battles, is described as an "unsung Northern hero of the South." These are the words of the author, not of any records keepers. It should be easy for the reader to distinguish the author's selective comments about the ninety-nine officers and men from the listing of obvious facts.

Information from published sources is also included for the sketches of Brooks, Cunningham, Hays, Hopper, Metcalf, and Wall. Material on Ferrell, summarized in the epilogue, comes from his own answers to questions from *Tennessee Questionnaires,* second volume. The Brooks/Cunningham/Logan connection after the war was taken from Arthur C. Cole's *The Era of the Civil War, 1848-1870,* vol. 3, pp. 401–2, plus the September 28 and October 2, 1866, issues of the *Cairo Democrat.*

1. **Ables, Private Jeremiah.** State of Birth: Alabama. State of residency, 1861: Kentucky (Paducah, McCracken County). He enlisted at Union City, Tennessee, on June 5, 1861, and was engaged at the battles of Belmont, Shiloh, and Perryville. One of the last eleven company men still left in the army, Private Ables was captured while doing picket duty on May 23, 1863, at a time when the Fifteenth Tennessee was in camp at Tullahoma, Tennessee. As a prisoner of war at Louisville, he was exchanged within a few days. Declared unfit for further service by the Confederate Medical Review Board, Ables was discharged from the army at Nashville on June 24 of that same year.

2. **Baldwin, Private William L.** State of birth: Ohio. State of residency, 1861: Pennsylvania. Occupation: carpenter. He was one of six members of G Company to have been born and raised in the North (non-slave states). Along with his friend, J. G. Patterson, Private Baldwin enlisted at Union City on June 5, 1861. He was listed as present for duty at Belmont and Shiloh. Baldwin was also one of the eight members of G company to be permanently transferred to other units or assignments. The Pennsylvanian was detailed with the Miners and Sappers, May of 1862 to December of that same year before being detailed as a carpenter from December 1, 1862, to February 1, 1863. Detailed with the Miners and Sappers again between February 1863 and February 1864, he was discharged from the army in March of 1864.

3. **Bell, Private James.** State of birth: Virginia. State of residency, 1861: Illinois (Marion, Williamson County). Having registered June 5, 1861, at Union City, he was listed as present during the battles of Belmont and Shiloh. Private Bell did not re-enlist after his one-year term expired and was consequently discharged at Tupelo, Mississippi, on July 20, 1862.

4. **Betts, Private J. M.** State of birth: Missouri. State of residency, 1861: Kentucky (Mayfield, Graves County). After having enlisted on June 5, 1861, at Union City, Private Betts was declared unfit for service by the Medical Review Board. He was discharged from the army at Columbus, Kentucky on September 10, 1861.

5. **Blankenship, Private Spince.** State of birth: Indiana (Knox County). Date of birth: May 6, 1834. State of residency, 1861: Illinois (Carbondale, Jackson County). Occupation: farmer. Marital status: single. Ancestry: English. Religion: Baptist. He was one of the six members of the Southern Illinois Company to be born and raised in the Northern states. After enlisting at Union City on June 5, 1861, he saw combat action at Belmont, and then assisted his friend, Sergeant Frank Metcalf, in rallying the color-guard at Shiloh. The Southern Illinoisan was detailed as a nurse at the Confederate hospital in Lauderdale Springs, Mississippi, during May and June of 1862. When Metcalf was wounded at Perryville, Blankenship advanced with the Fifteenth Tennessee regimental colors at the head of Major John M. Wall's battalion in Lieutenant Colonel Thorndike Brooks' offensive movement against the Second Ohio Infantry at the Widow Gibson's Farm. The gallant Private Blankenship, as a member of the color-guard of both the Fifteenth Tennessee and the Fifteenth/Thirty-Seventh Tennessee Consolidated, was wounded in action at the battles of Perryville (October 8, 1862), Chickamauga (September 20, 1863), and Jonesboro (August 31, 1864). This unsung Northern hero of the South was hospitalized all three times and was finally released to the Invalid Corps at Richmond, Virginia on February 15, 1865. His war record is one of the best of any Confederate enlisted man to come out of Southern Illinois. Spince Blankenship later returned to his native Knox County, Indiana, where he married, raised a family, and operated a small farm.

6. **Brooks, Lieutenant Colonel Thorndike.** State of birth: Maryland (Baltimore). Date of birth: March 11, 1828. Parents: Chauncy Brooks and Marilla Phelps. State of residency, 1861: Illinois (Marion, Williamson County). Marital status: married (wife Mary), three children. Occupation: merchant, planter. Ancestry: English, Scotch-Irish. Religion: Presbyterian. After organizing a unit of thirty-four Southern Illinois Confederate volunteers at Marion in May of 1861, he enlisted, along with his compatriots, on June 5 at Union City, where his command of South-

ern Illinoisans and Western Kentuckians became G Company of the Fifteenth Tennessee Regiment Volunteer Infantry, a West Tennessee outfit. Elected captain of the unit on the same day as registration, Thorndike Brooks eventually commanded a company of ninety-nine officers and men. These officers and men came from Western Kentucky (thirty-six from McCracken and Graves County), Southern Illinois (thirty-four from Williamson and Jackson Counties), Middle Tennessee (twenty-three), East Tennessee (two), Pennsylvania (two), Missouri (one), and Minnesota (one). At the November 7, 1861, Battle of Belmont, Missouri Captain Brooks' command was one of only four companies of the regiment not to break and run to the rear during an encounter with the Southern Illinoisans of the Federal Thirty-First Illinois Infantry. On the first day of the Battle of Shiloh—April 6, 1862—Lieutenant Colonel Robert Charles Tyler of the Fifteenth was seriously wounded, while his second-in-command, Major John F. Hearn, was off on a separate assignment. Before being seriously wounded himself, Brigadier General Bushrod R. Johnson bestowed temporary field command of the regiment on Captain Brooks. Brooks' unheralded twelve-minute stand on the Confederate left with the Fifteenth Tennessee and a remnant of the Second Tennessee (Irish) paved the way for a mid-morning Southern victory against the Union right, which was held down by the division of Major General William T. Sherman. Both the regiment and the company (known in the army as the Southern Illinois Company) sustained heavy casualties at Shiloh. When the Fifteenth Tennessee was reorganized at Tupelo, Mississippi on May 11, 1862, Brooks passed up the rank of major by being elected as the regimental lieutenant colonel, second in command under Colonel Tyler. Tyler was laid up with his Shiloh wound until the fall of 1862, when he was appointed as an aide to the divisional staff of Major General Frank Cheatham. All this while Brooks served as field commander of the Fifteenth. At the October 8, 1862, Battle of Perryville, Kentucky Colonel Tyler commanded a demi-brigade of two regiments and one battery detached from the all-Tennessee brigade of Brigadier General Daniel S. Donelson. Lieutenant Colonel Brooks, the highest ranking Illinois resident in all of Confederate service, was still commanding the Fifteenth. During the assault of Donelson's other three regiments, Brooks and his troops of the Fifteenth Tennessee Infantry took the enemy position that had been held down by the Second Ohio Infantry. Wounded by a sharp-shooter outside of Murfreesboro, Tennessee, on the last day of 1862, the lieutenant colonel was listed as absent because of wounds until May of 1863, when he returned to the regiment as Tyler's top subordinate. On June 6, the Fifteenth was consolidated with the Thirty-Seventh Tennessee under Colonel Robert C. Tyler. The senior lieutenant colonel of the consolidated regiment was Robert Dudley Fraser of the Thirty-Seventh. Muster rolls for the two original regiments was kept separate and Brooks remained in command of the Fifteenth. Still suffering from his Murfreesboro wound, the Southern Illinoisan was put back on sick leave at Meridian, Mississippi, between July 1863 and February 1864. During this period of time Brooks expressed fears about the safety of his family at Marion, Williamson County, Illinois. He applied for and received a pass, so that his loved ones were able to join him at Dalton, Georgia, in the spring of 1864. The family consisted of Mrs. Mary Brooks, the three children, and the children's nanny, Amanda Barrow. In the fall of 1863 Tyler was placed in command of Brigadier General William B. Bate's brigade when Bate was promoted to division command. Colonel Tyler, who was seriously wounded at the Battle of Missionary Ridge, received the rank of brigadier general in 1864. When Tyler moved up the ladder, Colonel Fraser took command of the consolidated regiment, while Major John M. Wall, replacing the ailing Brooks, took command of the Fifteenth. Like Tyler, Fraser also went down with a wound on November 25, 1863, at Missionary Ridge, as Wall ably took temporary command of the Fifteenth/Thirty-Seventh Tennessee Consolidated Infantry. This is important in understanding why Brooks was never promoted to the full rank of colonel. Unlike Wall, Brooks commanded the Fifteenth but not the Fifteenth/Thirty-Seventh. When the man from Marion returned to active duty in February of 1864, Colonel Thomas Benton Smith (later a brigadier) was commanding the brigade of the handicapped Brigadier General Robert Charles Tyler. Colonel Dudley Fraser commanded the Fifteenth/Thirty-Seventh; Lieutenant Colonel Thorndike Brooks, assisted by Major John M. Wall (soon to be killed in action at the Battle of Atlanta), commanded the Fifteenth Tennessee half of the regiment with Lieutenant Colonel Rufus M. Tankesly commanding the Thirty-Seventh half. Brooks was one of only three members of the original G Company, and the only Southern Illinoisan, to make it all the way through the conflict from Belmont to Bentonville, surrendering with General Joseph E. Johnston and the Army of Tennessee at Greensboro, North Carolina, on April 26, 1865. He had been in field command of the Fifteenth Tennessee Infantry for most of the period between May 1862 and May 1865, remaining until the end as the highest ranking Illinois Confederate and the only Illinois resident to command a regiment in the Confederate States Army. Two months after the war ended, Lieutenant Colonel Thorndike Brooks, a paroled prisoner since May 13, signed an oath of allegiance to the United States and petitioned President Andrew Johnson for a pardon. Johnson granted the request one month later, quite possibly as a favor to Brooks' father, Chauncey, a Baltimore merchant, banker and philanthropist, who had cooperated with Johns Hopkins to establish the Baltimore and Ohio Railroad, of which the elder Brooks served as president. As soon as the presidential pardon was granted, the former Confederate lieutenant colonel returned to his father's Baltimore home, where he was reunited with his two brothers who had fought in the Union Army. (He had three other brothers.) At first destitute and unable to support his wife and three children, he eventually became a prosperous Baltimore merchant. In 1875, at the request of Illinois Senator John A. Logan, Thorndike Brooks publicly denied that Logan had provided inspiration or assistance to the Southern Illinois Company. The two men were friends from that time on. In the summer of 1889, two and a half years after the death of Logan, Brooks became a charter member of the Baltimore Camp, United Confederate Veterans. He died in his Baltimore home four years later at the age of sixty-five.

7. **Brown, Private William J.** State of birth: Kentucky. State of residency, 1861: Illinois (Marion, Williamson County). Private Brown enlisted at Union City on June 5, 1861, and was then listed as present for duty at the Battle of Belmont. Detailed with the baggage between January 1 and May 1 of 1862, he did not re-enlist after one year and was discharged from the army at Tupelo on July 20, 1862.

8. **Carmon, Private Charles F.** State of birth: Georgia. State of residency, 1861: Kentucky (Mayfield, Graves County). Having enlisted at Columbus on September 5, 1861, he was engaged at Belmont. The gallant Private Carmon was then mortally wounded in action at the Battle

of Shiloh on April 6, 1862, and died in a Macon, Kentucky, hospital on May 14 of that same year.

9. **Childers, Private J. M.** State of birth: Virginia. State of residency, 1861: Kentucky (Paducah, McCracken County). He enlisted June 5, 1861, at Union City and was placed on sick leave between August 1, 1861, and July 1, 1862. After returning to the company after this long absence, Private Childers was declared unfit by the Medical Review Board, being discharged at Tupelo on July 5.

10. **Cooper, Private J. J.** State of birth: Kentucky. State of residency, 1861: Tennessee (Knoxville, Knox County). He enlisted for A Company of the Fifteenth on June 5, 1861, at Union City and was one of nine Tennesseeans registered for A Company to be transferred to G Company on the following day at Jackson, Tennessee. Private Cooper, having been listed as present at Belmont, refused to advance with the company at Shiloh and deserted a month later.

11. **Cordor, Sergeant P. Timothy, Jr.** State of birth: Kentucky (Mayfield, Graves County). State of residency, 1861: Illinois (Carbondale, Jackson County). He enlisted, along with his father, at Union City on June 5, 1861. The younger Tim Cordor was elected as a sergeant that September at Columbus, thereby outranking his father who was elected as a corporal at the same time. Sergeant Cordor was engaged at the Battle of Belmont. At Shiloh the gallant Tim, Jr., helped to rescue both his wounded father and the regimental colors. Possibly distraught by the death of his father a week after Shiloh, he did not re-enlist after one year and was subsequently discharged from the army on July 20, 1862.

12. **Cordor, Corporal P. Timothy, Sr.** State of birth: Mississippi. State of residency, 1861: Illinois (Carbondale, Jackson County). He enlisted, along with his son, on June 5, 1861, at Union City. At Columbus in September, Tim Sr. was elected as a corporal at the same time that his son was elected as a sergeant. He was placed on sick leave from November 1, 1861, to February 1, 1862. Rallying around the regimental colors the gallant Corporal Cordor was mortally wounded as his son helped him off the battlefield at Shiloh on April 6, 1862. He died on April 13.

13. **Cree, Corporal Samuel.** State of birth: Tennessee. State of residency, 1861: Kentucky (Paducah, McCracken County). After enlisting at Union City on June 5, 1861, he was placed on sick leave from August 16 to

October 31, 1861. Private Cree was wounded in action at Belmont, November 7, 1861, and was elected as a corporal shortly after. Battle wounds forced him to again be listed with the sick between January 1 and May 1, 1862. Corporal Cree returned to duty that May but deserted two months later.

14. **Cunningham, Captain Hibert A.** State of birth: Virginia. Date of birth: February 8, 1836. State of residency, 1861: Illinois (Marion, Williamson County). Occupation: planter. Marital status: single. Ancestry: Irish. Religion: Methodist. "Hibe" Cunningham was the brother-in-law of Major General John A. "Black Jack" Logan, a native of Jackson County, Illinois and the best high-ranking civilian soldier in Union service. One of the original Twelve Apostles and organizers of the Southern Illinois Confederate volunteers, Hibe enlisted at Union City on June 5, 1861, being elected as the first lieutenant of G Company on that same day. Two months later Lieutenant Cunningham performed his duties as a line officer by assisting Captain Thorndike Brooks of the Southern Illinois Company at Belmont, where Brooks' partly Southern Illinois command, G company of the Fifteenth Tennessee Infantry, was confronted by Logan's mostly Southern Illinois command, the Thirty-First Illinois Infantry. Cunningham was also engaged at Shiloh, where his performance was judged by Brooks to be erratic. The young Southern Illinois lieutenant tended to be insubordinate toward superior officers and discontented with his role in the army. When Thorndike Brooks was elected as the lieutenant colonel of the Fifteenth at the May 11, 1862 reorganization in Tupelo, the dashing Hibert A. Cunningham, popular with the enlisted men, was elected to replace him as G Company commander with the corresponding rank of captain. At Perryville on October 8, 1862, Captain Cunningham led a company-sized "battalion" of about one-hundred men that was the remnant of four companies of the Fifteenth, including the Southern Illinois Company. His advance was painfully slow and his own personal position on the battlefield was unknown. Late that afternoon, Cunningham's command, finally coming up from the rear, overran and captured two exposed guns of the Nineteenth Battery, Indiana Light Artillery. The rest of his Confederate military career is shrouded in mystery. At the start of the Tullahoma campaign, Captain Cunningham requested and received a furlough from June 1 to September 1, 1863. He

never returned to the army. Between September 15, 1863, and February 1, 1864, he was listed as AWOL. In February of 1864 he was officially branded as a deserter. In reality his fate had been sealed long before that. In the summer of 1863 Hibert A. Cunningham walked into his brother-in-law's tent and requested a Federal commission. With the rank of captain in the Union Army, Cunningham served on Logan's staff as an aide-de-camp during the Atlanta campaign. One of the enemy outfits during that tour of duty was the Fifteenth/Thirty-Seventh Tennessee. After the war Cunningham, like Logan, was held in contempt by most Southerners. But there are unusual circumstances about the man who held the rank of captain in both armies. Mary Cunningham Logan insisted that her younger brother joined up with the Confederate Army only because he was encouraged to do so by her husband. There is a good deal of evidence that suggests that Logan did, indeed, leave a strong impression with many of his constituents in Egypt that he was going south to fight at the head of a Southern Illinois Confederate regiment. The former congressman wavered between North and South, as he did during all of his early life, before declaring for the Union at Marion a full four months after Fort Sumter fell. Political ambition was certainly one of the reasons why Logan swung his sentiments toward the North. The loss of Logan and his many followers was definitely a blow to the Southern cause. Historians are left to ponder what would have happened in the Southern Illinois of 1861 if Jack Logan had declared for the Confederacy as Hibe Cunningham had expected. In 1878 the former captain in both armies, who had lived for some years in the state of Mississippi, traveled from his Williamson County, Illinois, home to Washington, D.C., for a prearranged visit with his brother-in-law and another man whom he had not seen in many years. The gentleman in question was Baltimore merchant Thorndike Brooks. Through the intercession of Logan, Brooks, and Cunningham achieved reconciliation and became friends as they had been seventeen years earlier in Marion. Because of Brooks' solid connection to both Confederate and Union veterans, Cunningham's good reputation was restored. When Thorndike Brooks died in 1893, Hibe Cunningham served as a pallbearer at the funeral. The Southern Illinois lawyer himself died two years later at the age of sixty.

15. **Cyerpit, Private William.** State of birth: North Carolina. State of residency, 1861: Tennessee (Hardin County). Occupation: blacksmith. Description: 5 feet 6 inches, light complexion, blue eyes, dark hair. After enlisting on June 5, 1861, at Union City, Private Cyerpit was engaged at Belmont. He was then one of six members of G company to be captured at Shiloh on April 6, 1862. After all six were exchanged shortly after the battle, they were discharged from the Confederate Army sometime between May and July of 1862. No dates are listed. More than likely the six did not re-enlist after their one year term expired. If this was the case, Cyerpit was discharged with the others at Tupelo on July 20 of that year.

16. **Davis, Private W. J.** State of birth: Ohio. State of residency, 1861: Illinois (Marion, Williamson County). Private W. J. Davis was one of only six members of the company to have been born and raised in the North. Having registered at Union City on June 5, 1861, he was engaged at Belmont. At Shiloh on April 6, 1862, this gallant Northerner gave his life for his adopted country.

17. **Davis, Private W. M.** State of birth: Tennessee. Date of birth: July 2, 1839. State of residency, 1861: Tennessee (Nashville, Davidson County). Occupation: farmer. Description: 5 feet 6 inches, dark complexion, black eyes, black hair. He was one of only two Tennessee residents of G Company to actually have been born in the Volunteer State. Enlisting on June 5, 1861, at Union City, this Nashville Tennessean was engaged at Belmont before being wounded at Shiloh. Due to his battle wounds, the gallant Private W. M. Davis was hospitalized in Meridian, Mississippi until July 20, 1862. Being partly disabled he did not re-enlist after his one year term expired and was discharged at Meridian on August 10 of that same year.

18. **Dillard, Private A. J.** State of birth: Louisiana. State of residency, 1861: Kentucky (Mayfield Graves County). He enlisted June 5, 1861 at Union City and was subsequently engaged at both Belmont and Shiloh. The gallant Private Dillard was killed in action by musketry fire from the Second Ohio Infantry at the Battle of Perryville, Kentucky on October 8, 1862.

19. **Dodson, Sergeant George H.** State of birth: Kentucky. State of residency, 1861: Illinois (Marion, Williamson County). After having enlisted at Union City on June 5, 1861, he was engaged at Belmont and

Shiloh. While the company was camped at Corinth, Mississippi, on May 15, 1862, this Southern Illinoisan was elected as a sergeant at the same time that E. Y. Eaker was being elected as a corporal. Thirteen days later Sergeant Dodson deserted along with Corporal Eaker.

20. **Dudley, Private B. A.** State of birth: Tennessee. State of residency, 1861: Kentucky (Paducah, McCracken County). He enlisted at Union City, June 5, 1861. Private Dudley became one of the eight members of G company to be permanently transferred to other assignments or units when he was detailed to Jackson's Battery of Artillery on January 1, 1862, and was then transferred to Cobb's Battery of Artillery later that year on June 11.

21. **Eaker, Corporal E. Y.** State of birth: Missouri. State of residency, 1861: Kentucky (Paducah, McCracken County). Enlisting at Union City on June 5, 1861, he participated in the battles of Belmont and Shiloh. On May 15, 1862, at Corinth, Private Eaker was elected as a corporal at the same time that George H. Dodson was being elected as a sergeant. Thirteen days later, Eaker and Dodson, assigned to the same picket detachment, deserted together.

22. **Ferrell, Private Calvin Henderson.** State of birth: Tennessee (Dyer County). Date of birth: March 29, 1838. State of residency, 1861: Tennessee (Stewart County). Occupation: farmer. Description: 6 feet, dark complexion, dark hair, hazel eyes, of Irish-born parents. Religion: Methodist. One of only two company Tennesseans to have been born in the state of Tennessee, he enlisted June 5, 1861, at Union City. After having been engaged at Belmont, Private Ferrell became one of six members of G company to be captured during the advance of the Fifteenth Tennessee at Shiloh and then exchanged shortly after, although no date is listed for the transfer of prisoners. Instead of re-enlisting with the Southern Illinois Company, he requested and received permission to transfer to A Company of Colonel Tyree H. Bell's Twelfth Tennessee Infantry, so that he could serve with his fellow Dyer County Tennesseans, thus becoming one of eight members of G Company to be permanently transferred to other assignments or units. Ferrell served honorably with the Twelfth until the close of the war, briefly residing at Atlanta, Georgia before returning to his native Dyer county. From 1865 to 1873 he successfully operated a mercantile business and then bought a farm and started a

nursery business. In 1887 Calvin Henderson Ferrell founded and became president of the Merchants State Bank at Humboldt, Tennessee (Dyer County). Believed to have been the last surviving member of G Company of the Fifteenth Tennessee Infantry, he was still alive, well, and active in 1922 at the age of eighty-four. As of this writing the date of his death has not been established from any of the newspapers of that era.

23. **Finnegan, Private John.** State of birth: Virginia. State of residency, 1861: Illinois (Marion, Williamson County). Like Private Calvin Henderson Ferrell, Private John Finnegan was the son of Irish immigrants. Enlisting June 5, 1861, at Union City, he was engaged at Belmont and Shiloh. After a tour on sick leave from July 1 to August 31, 1862, Finnegan was wounded and captured at the October 8 Battle of Perryville, Kentucky. Sent to Camp Butler in Springfield, Illinois, he grew weak from his wounds. On March 4, 1863, Federal authorities sent the Southern Illinoisan down to U.S.A. General Hospital No. 2 at Lexington, Kentucky. Two days later the Union Medical Review Board reported that the Confederate patient was suffering from a gunshot wound to the right thigh. Returned to Camp Butler on March 11, John Finnegan signed a Parole Oath on that same day. The oath enabled him to leave and to return to the hospital without escort. He was listed as being on furlough from the hospital between May 1 and August 31, 1863. Finnegan was then issued clothing at Lexington on September 22 and again on October 6. For the rest of the war he volunteered his services as a nurse at various Federal hospitals, although he was never officially registered in the enemy army.

24. **Gifford, Private Henry.** State of birth: Kentucky. State of residency, 1861: Illinois (Marion, Williamson County). He enlisted on June 5, 1861, at Union City and was listed as present for duty at Belmont. On April 6, 1862, at Shiloh, Private Gifford refused to advance with the Southern Illinois Company; two days later he deserted.

25. **Gomand, Private Edward.** State of birth: Alabama. State of residency, 1861: Tennessee (Pulaski, Giles County). One of the most durable and committed members of G Company, he was enlisted on June 5, 1861, at Union City. The gallant Private Gomand participated in the battles of Belmont, Shiloh, Perryville, Hoover's Gap, Chickamauga, and Missionary Ridge. During the Atlanta campaign, the downstate Middle Tennessean was wounded and captured at the Battle of Jonesboro, Georgia on

August 31, 1864. He was exchanged on September 19 and released to the Invalid Corps.

26. **Goodridge, Private J. D.** State of birth: Tennessee. State of residency, 1861: Kentucky (Mayfield, Graves County). After enlisting at Union City on June 5, 1861, he was listed as present at Belmont. Private Goodridge was one of the six members of the company to be captured at Shiloh and then exchanged shortly after, no date being listed for the exchange. Apparently he did not re-enlist after his original one year term and was discharged at Tupelo on July 20, 1862.

27. **Gowins, Private Thomas.** State of birth: unknown. State of residency, 1861: (Kentucky, Graves County). Thomas Gowins was the most notorious member of G company, Fifteenth Tennessee Infantry. During the spring of 1861, he killed a citizen of Graves County, a certain Mr. J. Pryor. At the time he was killed by Gowins, Pryor himself was out on a five-thousand-dollar bond for killing a man. According to Gowins, he shot Pryor in self-defense, alleging that Pryor had chased him around with a double-barrel shotgun, threatening his life. Federal authorities offered Gowins his liberty if he would join the Union Army, but he declined. Failing to post a three-thousand-dollar bond, the Western Kentuckian was arrested and jailed but escaped. While a fugitive from justice Gowins joined up with the Southern Illinois and Western Kentucky volunteers of Captain Thorndike Brooks at Paducah, and then enlisted at Union City on June 5. Even if Thomas Gowins was indeed a scoundrel, at least it can be said that he was also a loyal Southern scoundrel. During the tour of duty at Columbus First Lieutenant John M. Wall, another resident of Graves County, heard rumors about Private Gowins and made inquiries. As the result of a December 17, 1861, letter from Dr. Wall to Brigadier General Gideon J. Pillow, Gowins was cashiered from the Confederate Army and handed over to Kentucky state authorities who, in turn, handed him over to the U.S. Marshal's office. Consequently he was arrested and jailed again—this time in Paducah. During this second incarceration, a guard detachment of Federal troops was threatening to remove him from jail and hang him. The story ends here in the Tennessee State Confederate Service Records. The final fate of Thomas Gowins is unknown.

28. **Graham, Sergeant Major Samuel H.** State of birth: unknown. State of residency, 1861: Minnesota. This twenty-eight-year-old Northerner

enlisted at Union City on June 5, 1861. Since the place of his birth is unknown, it cannot be determined if S. H. Graham had any previous connection to the South. It is certain that he was one of the most popular and courageous members of the company. Engaged at Belmont, the Minnesotan performed extremely well at Shiloh before being elected as the sergeant major of G company at Corinth on May 15, 1862. Sergeant Major Graham served with distinction throughout the Western campaigns, firing away at the enemy during the battles of Perryville, Hoover's Gap, Chickamauga, and Missionary Ridge. While on duty with the Fifteenth/Thirty-Seventh Tennessee during the Atlanta campaign, his skill with a musket caught the attention of his division commander, Major General William B. Bate. By special order from Bate himself, the Minnesota Confederate was placed on extra duty as a sharpshooter during General John Bell Hood's ill-fated advance into Federally-occupied Tennessee in September of 1864. Severely wounded in the neck by musketry fire at the November 30 Battle of Franklin, Tennessee, the gallant sergeant major lost a lot of blood before he could be assisted by the medical staff. He never fully recovered from his Franklin wounds, which were complicated by disease, thus giving his life for his adopted country. Sergeant Major Samuel H. Graham, a true unsung Southern patriot, died on January 12, 1865, and is interred at Franklin's McGavock Confederate Cemetery, grave number 11182, in the Tennessee section.

29. **Gray, Private John.** State of birth: South Carolina. State of residency, 1861: Tennessee (Hickman County.) Description: 6 feet 1 inch, light complexion, dark hair, blue eyes. Enlisting at Union City on June 5, 1861, he was engaged at Belmont. Private Gray was one of six members of G company to be captured at Shiloh and exchanged shortly after, the date of the exchange unknown. Most probably he did not re-enlist after one year and was discharged at Tupelo on July 20, 1862.

30. **Grayham, Private Lester.** State of birth: Kentucky. State of residency, 1861: Tennessee (Sumner County). He enlisted June 5, 1861, at Union City. On August 1, less than two months later, Private Grayham resigned from the army for unknown personal reasons.

31. **Gryder, Private J. L.** State of birth: Arkansas. State of residency, 1861: Tennessee (Nashville, Davidson County). After enlisting on August 28, 1861, at Island Number Ten, Tennessee, Private Gryder was on

the company active roster for exactly one day. According to medical reports, he was on sick leave from August 29, 1861, until March 31, 1863. On April 1, 1863, he was discharged because of his unspecified illness.

32. **Gunn, Private J. T.** State of birth: Virginia. State of residency, 1861: Kentucky (Mayfield, Graves County). This Western Kentuckian registered for G Company at Columbus on September 28, 1861, and was listed as present at Belmont. The gallant Private Gunn was mortally wounded in action at the Battle of Shiloh, April 6, 1862, dying of his wounds at the Confederate hospital in Lauderdale Springs, Mississippi precisely one week later, April 13.

33. **Harrington, Private George W.** State of birth: Kentucky. State of residency, 1861: Kentucky (Paducah, McCracken County). G. W. Harrington was the only Kentucky resident of G Company to actually have been born in the Bluegrass State. Enlisting at Union City on June 5, 1861, he was engaged at Belmont. On sick leave January 1 to May 1, 1862, he was detailed as a nurse at Lauderdale Springs May 1 to July 1, 1862. Sometime in July or August of that year at Tupelo, Private Harrington deserted.

34. **Hayes, Private J. T.** State of birth: Missouri. State of residency, 1861: Kentucky (Paducah, McCracken County). After having enlisted June 5, 1861, at Union City, he was listed as present at Belmont. On sick leave January 1 to June 1, 1862, Private Hayes was admitted to the Overton General Hospital in Memphis on March 12 of that same year. Due to an unknown illness he was discharged on June 1, 1862.

35. **Hays, Second Lieutenant Harvey L.** State of birth: Kentucky. Date of birth: April 11, 1828. State of residency, 1861: Illinois (Marion, Williamson County). Occupation: planter. Marital status: married, no information about children. Ancestry: Irish. Religion: Baptist. One of the original Twelve Apostles and organizers of the Southern Illinois volunteers, Harvey Hays enlisted on June 5, 1861. At Union City on that same day he was elected as the Brevet Second Lieutenant of G company, the fourth ranking officer of the unit, behind fellow Williamson County Southern Illinoisans Thorndike Brooks, Hibert A. Cunningham, and Henry C. Hopper. Because of the fact that all four company officers were from the Marion area, Confederate Service Records (CSR) began to refer to this unit as the Southern Illinois Company. Hays, a hard-drinking

soldier, performed well rallying the men in pursuit of enemy troops at Belmont, November 7, 1861. At the April 6, 1862, Battle of Shiloh he demonstrated considerable courage in the face of a Federal artillery barrage in spite of being drunk. Because of his steadiness under fire at both Belmont and Shiloh, the men of G Company elected him to the permanent rank of second lieutenant during the reorganization in Mississippi, a move that officially made him a Confederate commissioned officer. Unfortunately the military career of Second Lieutenant Harvey L. Hays had an extremely abrupt and sad ending. As a result of a series of drunken disputes with other officers and men, Lieutenant Colonel Robert C. Tyler of the Fifteenth Tennessee felt compelled, for the betterment of the service, to relieve the hot-tempered Southern Illinoisan from duty on May 15, 1862, the very same day as his promotion. A month later the company lost one of its toughest combat officers when Harvey Hays was cashiered from the army, his drinking and perhaps his life out of control. Apparently he never returned to Southern Illinois, but all postwar records for him are presently missing.

36. **Haywood, Private W. W.** State of birth: Virginia (Richmond). Date of birth: May 14, 1802. State of residency, 1861: Tennessee (Nashville, Davidson County). Description: 5 feet 5 inches, dark complexion, blue eyes, black hair. He enlisted June 5, 1861, at Union City after having been certified by the Medical Review Board as being in "excellent condition." In spite of his advanced age (fifty-nine) W. W. Haywood was elected as the original drummer of the company. He ably served in that capacity at both Belmont and Shiloh. While pounding out the retirement at Shiloh on April 6, 1862, the gallant Private Haywood was disabled for life by fragments from an exploding shell that lodged in his legs, thighs, and back. The oldest member of the Fifteenth Tennessee Infantry was discharged because of his disability on June 18, 1862, thirty-five days after his sixtieth birthday.

37. **Holland, Private Bryce.** State of birth: Virginia. State of residency, 1861: Tennessee (Davidson County). After having enlisted for G Company on August 28, 1861, at Island Number Ten, he was listed as present for duty at Columbus. His whereabouts during the battles of Belmont and Shiloh are unknown. Private Holland deserted at Tupelo sometime in July or August of 1862.

38. **Holmes, Private Titus.** State of birth: Maryland. State of residency, 1861: Kentucky (Paducah, McCracken County). He enlisted at Union City on June 5, 1861. The strange case of Private Titus Holmes is even stranger than the strange case of Private Bryce Holland. Holmes was never listed under any military classification, not even "present." His presence within the army could not be verified at all except for the fact that he deserted at Corinth on May 28, 1862.

39. **Hopper, First Lieutenant Henry C.** State of birth: Tennessee (Brentwood, Williamson County). Date of birth: January 26, 1824. State of residency, 1861: Illinois (Marion, Williamson County). Occupation: telegraph operator. Marital status: widower, five children. Ancestry: Anglo-Irish. Religion: Episcopalian. Harry Hopper was, so to speak, the "Founding Father" of the Twelve Apostles and one of the organizers of the Southern Illinois volunteers. It was his "resolutions" that prompted Colonel B. M. Prentiss to send troops of the Tenth Illinois Infantry to "quell the uprising" at Carbondale. Having enlisted on June 5, 1861, at Union City, he took an active part as a line officer at the battles of Belmont and Shiloh, although he did not distinguish himself. At the reorganization of G Company at Corinth on May 15, 1862, Harry was promoted from second lieutenant to first lieutenant when his fellow Southern Illinoisan, Hibe Cunningham, moved up the ladder from first lieutenant to captain. In this capacity he did not serve very long. First Lieutenant Hopper was placed on sick leave between July 1, 1862, and January 1, 1863, missing the action at Perryville and Murfreesboro. He did return to the Fifteenth Tennessee in January before resigning for personal reasons on March 14, 1863. In his letter of resignation, Henry C. Hopper, a widower, stated that his mother who had been caring for his five children had recently died, necessitating his return home. Issued clothing and discharged from the army on that same day, he traveled back up to Williamson County, Illinois. After the war, he moved his residency to Graves County, Kentucky.

40. **Hudgens, Second Lieutenant Bryant W.** State of birth: Tennessee (Robertson County). Date of birth: June 13, 1841. State of residency, 1861: Tennessee (Cheatham County). Occupation: farmer, son of a preacher. Marital status: single. Ancestry: English. Religion: Baptist. B. W. Hudgens was one of only two members among the Tennessee residents

of G Company to have also been born in the state of Tennessee. He enlisted for A Company of the Fifteenth Tennessee Infantry at Union City on June 5, 1861, and on the following day at Jackson he became one of the nine members of A Company to be transferred to G Company. He fought with distinction at Belmont and Shiloh. Shortly after the May 15, 1862, reorganization of the company at Corinth the youthful but highly respected Middle Tennessean was elected as the second lieutenant, replacing the irascible Harvey Hays who had been relieved of his command. He was the second of only two commissioned officers of the Southern Illinois Company to come from outside the state of Illinois. Second Lieutenant Hudgens led the remnant of the company in Captain Hibert A. Cunningham's one-hundred-man battalion at the Battle of Perryville. It was Hudgens who rallied and led the whole command in the absence of Cunningham. The second lieutenant began to lose his eyesight early in 1863, a disease identified by the Medical Review Board as erysipelas of the orbits. Because of his handicap, the young officer was assigned to the Conscription Service between May 1, 1863, and October 1, 1864. During part of this time, he was confined to the Confederate hospital at Macon, Georgia. After declining a disability discharge, the gallant Hudgens returned to the Fifteenth/Thirty-Seventh Tennessee as a staff officer for Colonel R. Dudley Fraser, being listed as present for duty during the battles of Franklin, Nashville, and Bentonville. Surrendering with the Army of Tennessee at Greensboro, North Carolina on April 26, 1865, he was one of only three members of G company to make it all the way through four years of war, beginning to end. As a company officer his military record is surpassed by only Thorndike Brooks and John M. Wall. Following his May 13 parole, twenty-three-year-old Bryant W. Hudgens went home to Cheatham County, where he served as a preacher. Nearly totally blind he became one of the two members of the company to receive a veterans pension from the state of Tennessee (File No. 3281).

41. **Hunter, Private E. C.** State of birth: Tennessee. State of residency, 1861: Kentucky (Mayfield, Graves County). He enlisted for G Company on October 8, 1861, at Columbus. On detached guard duty at the Columbus garrison during the November 7 Battle of Belmont, Private E. C. Hunter was seriously wounded at Shiloh on April 6, 1862, and, as a result, was placed on medical leave between May 1, 1862, and January 31,

1863. Declared unfit for service by the Medical Review Board, the gallant Western Kentuckian was discharged because of his wounds on February 1, 1863.

42. **Hunter, Private L. A.** State of birth: Kentucky. State of residency, 1861: Tennessee (Wilson County). After enlisting for A Company at Union City on June 5, 1861, he was transferred from A to G at Jackson on June 6. This Middle Tennessean was on sick leave August 11 to November 1, 1861, before being listed as "not stated" for both Belmont and Shiloh. It was reported that Private L. A. Hunter lost or abandoned his weapons and equipment on the march from Corinth to Tupelo. On June 26, 1862, he deserted.

43. **Jenkins, Private Fred A.** State of birth: Georgia. State of residency, 1861: Kentucky (Paducah, McCracken County). He enlisted June 5, 1861, at Union City. The role of the Fifteenth Tennessee at Belmont was to pursue a badly beaten foe. In spite of this Private Jenkins of G Company was the only member of the entire regiment to be captured, a highly suspicious event. He was, at first, listed by the Northerners as a prisoner of war at Keysburg, Kentucky before being transferred to Vicksburg, Mississippi by Federal authorities on November 11, 1861. He was exchanged in January but deserted the Confederate Army near Shiloh on April 12, 1862. Jenkins became the first of only two members of the company to formally betray his country when he registered for Union service at Vicksburg on November 15, 1862.

44. **Jent, Private Flemming.** State of birth: Kentucky. State of residency, 1861: Illinois (Marion, Williamson County). He enlisted at Union City on June 5, 1861, and was listed as present at Belmont and Shiloh. Detailed as a teamster on July 1, 1862, Private Jent failed to show up at his new assignment. One month later, on August 1, he was officially listed as a deserter and was never seen again.

45. **Johnson, Private Joshua B.** State of birth: South Carolina. State of residency, 1861: Tennessee (Montgomery County). Occupation: telegraph operator. After having enlisted for A Company of the Fifteenth Tennessee at Union City on June 5, 1861, Private J. B. Johnson and eight others were transferred to G Company the following day at Jackson. On detached service from September 21 to December 30, 1861, he became one of eight members of the company to be permanently transferred to other units or

assignments when he was detailed to work as a telegraph operator at Camp Lee, Hardeville, South Carolina. The appointment was dated January 9, 1862, to last for two years. During this detail the Upper Middle Tennessean spent six months on sick leave. He was discharged from the army on January 1, 1864.

46. **Jones, Private S. T.** State of birth: Tennessee. State of residency, 1861: Kentucky (Mayfield, Graves County). He enlisted on June 5, 1861, at Union City and was listed as present for duty at Columbus. At the April 6, 1862, Battle of Shiloh, Private Jones refused to advance with the company and deserted near Corinth on May 3, 1862.

47. **Kelly, Sergeant Robert R.** State of birth: Illinois (Marion, Williamson County). Date of birth: December 26, 1842. State of residency, 1861: Illinois (Marion, Williamson County). Occupation: farmer. Marital status: married. Ancestry: Irish. Religion: Episcopalian. R. R. Kelly was one of only six members of G Company to have been born and raised in the North and the only member of the Southern Illinois volunteers to have been born in the state of Illinois. Oddly enough, he was also the lone member of G Company to have lived his entire life in the same county of the same state. He enlisted at Union City on June 5, 1861. At the time of the company organization the likeable and responsible Southern Illinois youngster was elected as a sergeant and appointed by Captain Brooks to be an assistant quartermaster. In that capacity he requisitioned seventy-five pair of socks. Almost immediately after this Sergeant Kelly was informed by a letter from home that his teenaged bride had taken ill. He requested a resignation for personal reasons, and it was granted on August 18, 1861. It is happily reported that Mr. and Mrs. Kelly lived many years and had several children. Before he left for home Kelly dutifully passed the socks down to his successor, Samuel H. Graham, who in turn distributed them to the men in need. Farmer Kelly continued to live in Williamson County where he raised a large family.

48. **Klein, Private Calvin R.** State of birth: Missouri. State of residency, 1861: Kentucky (Paducah, McCracken County). He enlisted for G Company at Union City on June 5, 1861. As a noncombatant this Western Kentuckian was detailed to the Commissary Sergeant, November 20 to December 30, 1861, and was then attached to the Noncommissioned Officers Staff, January 1 to May 1, 1862. After being on sick leave May 1

to 31, Private Klein was discharged from the army because of sickness on June 1 of that year.

49. **Knight, Private Daniel.** State of birth: Mississippi. State of residency, 1861: Tennessee (Bedford County). Having enlisted for A Company at Union City on June 5, 1861, he became one of nine members of that company to be transferred to G Company at Jackson on June 6. Temporarily detached as a teamster at Columbus September 15, 1861, to January 31, 1862, the Middle Tennessean was seriously wounded at the April 6, 1862, Battle of Shiloh. Because of his wound the gallant Private Knight was placed on sick leave from May 1, 1862, until February 1, 1863. The Medical Review Board declared him disabled, and he was subsequently discharged sometime in March or April of 1863.

50. **Kyle, Private J. C.** State of birth: Virginia. State of residency, 1861: Illinois (Marion, Williamson County). He enlisted on June 5, 1861, at Union City and was listed as present at both Belmont and Shiloh. On July 14, 1862, the Medical Review Board declared Private Kyle unfit for service because of obesity and old age. He was immediately discharged.

51. **Lewelling, Private J. W.** State of birth: Delaware. State of residency, 1861: Tennessee (Maury County). Along with eight others he enlisted at Union City on June 5, 1861, and was then transferred from A Company to G Company the following day at Jackson. He was listed as present for duty at Belmont and Shiloh. Shortly after the reorganization at Corinth in May of 1862, Private Lewelling deserted.

52. **Lowe, Private A. J.** State of birth: Tennessee. State of residency, 1861: Illinois (Marion, Williamson County). Having enlisted June 5, 1861, at Union City he was listed as *not* present at Belmont, after which he refused to advance at Shiloh. On April 28, 1862, during the withdrawal of Confederate troops from Pittsburg Landing down to Corinth, Private A. J. Lowe deserted.

53. **Lowe, Corporal Joshua.** State of birth: Kentucky. State of residency, 1861: Tennessee (Marshall County). Enlisting at Island Number Ten on August 28, 1861, he was engaged at both Belmont and Shiloh. At the reorganization of G Company at Corinth on May 15, 1862, Private Joshua Lowe was elected as a corporal. On June 1 he was granted a thirty day personal leave. This Middle Tennessean returned to duty in July but did

not re-enlist after his original one year term expired, being discharged from the army at Tupelo on August 11, 1862.

54. **Lyle, Private Richard.** State of birth: Texas. State of residency, 1861: Tennessee (Davidson County). He enlisted at Union City on June 5, 1861, and was then engaged at Belmont. Private Lyle was captured at Shiloh on April 6, 1862, and sent to Camp Douglas, Chicago. It is not known why he was not exchanged along with the other seven prisoners of G company. On August 30, 1862, at Camp Douglas he took the Oath of Allegiance to the United States and went home.

55. **Mason, Private John.** State of birth: Tennessee. State of residency, 1861: Kentucky (Paducah, McCracken County). After enlisting on June 5, 1861, at Union City, he was engaged at Belmont and Shiloh. Private Mason did not re-enlist after his one year hitch and was discharged at Tupelo on July 20, 1862.

56. **McClartney, Sergeant John.** State of birth: Missouri. State of residency, 1861: Kentucky (Paducah, McCracken County). The Irish-American enlisted at Union City on June 5, 1861. Listed as present at Belmont, he was then listed as "killed in action" at Shiloh on April 6, 1862. The report about his death was, however, greatly exaggerated. At the reorganization of the Southern Illinois Company at Corinth on May 15 of that same year, this Western Kentuckian was elected as a sergeant. Therefore it is highly unlikely that he was dead. The fact that Sergeant McClartney was still breathing was established with certainty during July of 1862, when he deserted.

57. **McGeehee, Private D. L. L.** State of birth: Missouri. State of residency, 1861: Kentucky (Mayfield, Graves County). He enlisted on September 10, 1861, at Columbus but was listed as *not* present at Belmont. Private McGeehee deserted from the army on March 9, 1862, by jumping off a transport on the Mississippi River somewhere between Columbus, Kentucky and Memphis, Tennessee.

58. **McKensie, Private Alex.** State of birth: Missouri (Cape Giradeau). Date of birth: May 19, 1824. State of residency, 1861: Illinois (Marion, Williamson County). Occupation: stonemason. Description: 6 feet 3 inches, dark complexion, gray eyes, dark hair. Registering on June 5, 1861, at Union City, this tall man was listed as present for duty at Belmont. After being detailed as a teamster at Columbus between January 1 and

February 28, 1862, he returned to active duty in G Company that March, after which he was listed as present at Shiloh. Private McKensie did not re-enlist after one year and, as a result, was discharged at Tupelo on July 20, 1862.

59. **McKinelly, Private A. R.** State of birth: Tennessee. State of residency, 1861: Illinois (Marion, Williamson County). He enlisted at Union City on June 5, 1861. The gallant Private McKinelly was wounded the following November 7 at the Battle of Belmont, but was then reported to be "not stated" at Shiloh. More than likely he was still laid up with his Belmont wound. It is not known if the wound caused a disability. Although this Southern Illinoisan is not listed on any hospital records, this could well be an oversight. In any case he did not re-enlist after his initial term and was discharged from the army on July 20, 1862, at Tupelo.

60. **Metcalf, Sergeant Frank.** Place of birth: Canada. Date of birth: August 3, 1836. Raised in: Kentucky (Mayfield, Graves County). State of residency, 1861: Illinois (Carbondale, Jackson County). Occupation: farmer. Description: 5 feet 8 inches, dark complexion, black eyes, dark hair. Marital status: married, two children. Ancestry: Canadian, English. Religion: Methodist. It was Frank Metcalf who recruited the other five Jackson County members of Captain Brooks' thirty-four Southern Illinois volunteers. His enlistment took place at Union City on June 5, 1861. On the following day at the Jackson, Tennessee training camp, Metcalf was elected as a sergeant for G Company of the Fifteenth Tennessee Infantry. Sergeant Metcalf, for a period of eleven months that included three major battles, had the most outstanding service record of any of the company's enlisted men. At Belmont on November 7, 1861, he was cited for distinguished service by Captain Thorndike Brooks, although his meritorious deeds remain unknown. At Shiloh on the first day—April 6, 1862—Sergeant Metcalf commanded an improvised squadron consisting of all six Jackson County men, including himself. During the early Federal bombardment, the Carbondale Confederate was credited by Brooks with holding the line of both the Fifteenth and Second (Irish) Tennessee regiments by rallying the men around the colors of the Fifteenth. When the reorganization of the Southern Illinois Company was held at Corinth, Mississippi on May 15, Frank Metcalf was transferred to the regimental staff and given the honor of becoming the standard-bearer of

the Fifteenth. During the advance of the Fifteenth and Sixteenth Tennessee regiments at Perryville, Kentucky on October 8 of that same year, this gallant Southern Illinoisan protected the battle flag from capture in spite of being wounded in four places by enemy canister. His friend and compatriot, Private Spince Blankenship, then took possession of the flag pole. Declared medically unfit for service by the Medical Review Board because of his wounds, Sergeant Metcalf was transferred to the Invalid Corps on October 29, 1862. Following the conflict he moved his family back to his boyhood home of Mayfield in Graves County, Kentucky, where he was reunited with several other veterans of G Company, most notably Harry Hopper. There he wrote about the organization of the Southern Illinois Confederate volunteers. Frank Metcalf, an unsung hero of the South, died in his Western Kentucky home on October 6, 1917—two days shy of fifty-five years after he had suffered multiple wounds defending the colors at Perryville. He was eighty-one years old.

61. **Meyer, Sergeant W. J.** State of birth: South Carolina. State of residency, 1861: Kentucky (Paducah, McCracken County). He enlisted on June 5, 1861 and was assigned to G Company, Fifteenth Tennessee at Union City. While serving with the company, the South Carolina native was a noncombatant from start to finish. After having been attached to the Noncommissioned Officers Staff from January 1 until May 1 of 1862, he was detailed as a wagon master, May 1 to June 1. Assigned back with the Noncommissioned Officers Staff June 1, 1862, to June 1, 1863, he had already been appointed as a sergeant on April 1, 1863. Sergeant Meyer became one of the eight members of G Company to be permanently transferred to other assignments or units on July 1, 1863, when he was sent to the South Carolina Heavy Artillery.

62. **Moore, Private Isreal.** State of birth: Virginia. State of residency, 1861: Tennessee (Dickson County). Description: 5 feet 7 inches, light complexion, auburn hair, gray eyes. Following his registration at Union City on June 5, 1861, he was listed as present for duty at both Belmont and Shiloh. Private Moore did not re-enlist after one year and was discharged at Tupelo on July 20, 1862. He later made his home in Obion County, northwestern Tennessee.

63. **Morgan, Private A. H.** State of birth: Tennessee. State of residency, 1861: Kentucky (Mayfield, Graves County). He enlisted June 5, 1861,

at Union City. Permanently disabled by musketry fire at the November 7, 1861, Battle of Belmont, the gallant Private Morgan was listed as "wounded with leave" between December 1, 1861, and May 1, 1862. He was subsequently declared unfit for service by the Medical Review Board and discharged from the army on August 18, 1862.

64. **Morris, Private Asa G.** State of birth: Georgia. State of residency, 1861: Tennessee (Nashville, Davidson County). After enlisting for A Company of the Fifteenth Tennessee on June 5, 1861, at Union City, A. G. Morris was one of nine members of A Company to be transferred to G Company at Jackson on June 6. One of the most dependable enlisted men of the Southern Illinois Company, he was engaged at both Belmont and Shiloh. Private Morris may have been wounded at the latter but it cannot be assumed with certainty. After being sick with leave from May 1 to June 30 of 1862, he returned to the company and was engaged at Perryville and Hoover's Gap. Critically wounded by dismounted Federal troopers at Reed's Bridge on September 18, 1863, during the Chickamauga Campaign, Asa G. Morris was confined to two Confederate hospitals for a period of one year, first in Atlanta, then in Savannah. In October 1864, this gallant Middle Tennessean was assigned to the Invalid Corps.

65. **Mowlen, Private James.** State of birth: North Carolina. State of residency, 1861: Tennessee (Murfreesboro, Rutherford County). Enlisting September 1, 1861, at Island Number Ten, the Middle Tennessean was engaged at Belmont. The gallant Private Mowlen was mortally wounded in action at the Battle of Shiloh, April 6, 1862. Left on the battlefield during the retirement of the Fifteenth Tennessee, he died a few hours later.

66. **Mullens, Private Robert.** State of birth: Missouri. State of residency, 1861: Kentucky (Paducah, McCracken County). His enlistment took place at Union City on June 5, 1861. Although next to nothing is known about him, Private Mullens was certainly one of the most durable enlisted men of G Company. This gallant Western Kentuckian was one of only three members of the company to participate in all of the campaigns from Belmont to Bentonville before surrendering with the Army of Tennessee at Greensboro, North Carolina, on April 26, 1865.

67. **Ogle, Private Frank.** State of birth: Kentucky. State of residency, 1861: Tennessee (Humphreys County). Following his June 5, 1861 reg-

istration at Union City, he was listed as present at Belmont and Shiloh. Private Ogle had the rare distinction of being imprisoned by both the Confederates and the Federals. At the beginning of the 1863 Tullahoma campaign he was held back in the stockade at Knoxville for some unknown offense. For a fifty-dollar bounty he was released and allowed to rejoin the Fifteenth/Thirty-Seventh Tennessee at Chattanooga. During the Atlanta campaign, the Middle Tennessean was captured at the Battle of Kennesaw Mountain on June 27, 1864. Sent to Camp Morton, Indiana, he was released after the war.

68. **Parkhill, Private J. F.** State of birth: unknown. State of residency, 1861: Kentucky (Paducah, McCracken County). Having registered on June 5, 1861, at Union City, he was listed as present for Belmont. Private Parkhill was one of the seven members of G Company to run to the rear in panic at Shiloh on April 6, 1862. He deserted on May 3 of that year.

69. **Parton, Private Joseph.** State of birth: Alabama. State of residency, 1861: Tennessee (Giles County). After having enlisted for A Company at Union City on June 5, 1861, he was transferred, along with eight others, to G Company the next day at Jackson. He was then listed as present for duty at Belmont and Shiloh. Private Parton did not re-enlist after his hitch was up. At Tupelo on July 20, 1862, this South Middle Tennessean was discharged from the army.

70. **Patterson, Private G. L.** State of birth: Virginia. State of residency, 1861: Illinois (Marion, Williamson County). Enlisting June 5, 1861, at Union City he was engaged at the November 7, 1861, Battle of Belmont. The gallant G. L. Patterson, one of Captain Brooks' Southern Illinois recruits, gave his life for the South at Shiloh on April 6, 1862.

71. **Patterson, Private J. G.** State of birth: Ohio (Roscoe). Date of birth: August 28, 1823. State of residency, 1861: Pennsylvania. Occupation: carpenter. Description: fair complexion, blue eyes, dark hair. He was one of the six members of G Company to have been born and raised in the North. Along with his close personal friend, W. L. Baldwin, this Confederate Pennsylvanian enlisted at Union City on June 5, 1861, prior to seeing combat action at both Belmont and Shiloh. Detailed with the Sappers and Miners May 1, 1862, to December 30, 1863, Private J. G. Patterson was one of eight members of the company to be permanently transferred to other assignments or units on January 1, 1864, when he

was officially registered with the Sappers and Miners detachment in South Carolina, where he served for the remainder of the conflict.

72. **Patterson, Private John.** Place of birth: Ireland (County Antrim). Date of birth: November 17, 1826. State of residency, 1861: Kentucky (Paducah, McCracken County). The Irishman enlisted at Union City on June 5, 1861, and was engaged at Belmont on November 7 of that year. The only Irish-born member of G Company, the gallant Private John Patterson was wounded in the foot at Shiloh on April 6, 1862, spending the better part of the next three weeks in an ambulance. Still walking with a limp, he did not re-enlist after his initial tour of duty, being discharged from the army at Tupelo on July 15, 1862. After the war the Irishman moved from Western Kentucky to the town of Stantonville, McNairy County, just west of the Tennessee River and just above the Mississippi state border in West Tennessee, where he owned his family farm. He was one of only two members of the Southern Illinois Company of the Fifteenth Tennessee to receive a veterans pension from the state of Tennessee (File No. 4551).

73. **Payne, Private J. M.** State of birth: Tennessee. State of residency, 1861: Kentucky (Mayfield, Graves County). After having enlisted at Columbus on September 30, 1861, he was listed as present for duty at both Belmont and Shiloh. Private Payne did not re-enlist after one year and was discharged at Tupelo on July 20, 1862.

74. **Pentecost, Private F. A.** State of birth: Missouri. State of residency, 1861: Kentucky (Paducah, McCracken County). F. A. Pentecost was the cousin of W. T. Pentecost. He enlisted June 5, 1861, at Union City. Private F. A. Pentecost was declared unfit for service in early September by the Medical Review Board and was discharged on exactly the same day that his cousin enlisted, September 10, 1861.

75. **Pentecost, Private W. T.** State of birth: Missouri. State of residency, 1861: Kentucky (Mayfield, Graves County). W. T. Pentecost was the cousin of F. A. Pentecost. He enlisted at Columbus on the same day that his cousin was discharged, September 10, 1861. Precisely six days after his cousin left and he arrived, Private W. T. Pentecost was placed on sick leave. Two days later he became a rarity in the annals of American military history, deserting within forty-eight hours of being placed on sick leave and within eight days of enlistment.

76. **Perry, Corporal G. W.** State of birth: Virginia. State of residency, 1861: Illinois (Marion, Williamson County). Following his enlistment at Union City on June 5, 1861, he was engaged at Belmont and Shiloh. At the reorganization of G company at Corinth on May 15, 1862, Private Perry was elected as a corporal. Two weeks later he received permission for a one month furlough but never returned to the army. On August 1, 1862, he was officially listed as a deserter.

77. **Price, Private J. P.** State of birth: Kentucky. State of residency, 1861: Tennessee (Knoxville, Knox County). After enlisting for A Company at Union City on June 5, 1861, Private J. P. Price and eight others were transferred to G Company the following day at Jackson. He was present at Belmont but refused to advance at Shiloh, deserting shortly after.

78. **Randall, Private Calvin.** State of birth: Kentucky. Date of birth: October 24, 1836. State of residency, 1861: Illinois (Marion, Williamson County). Occupation: wagon maker. Description: 5 feet 7 inches, dark hair, dark eyes, dark complexion. Calvin Randall was the brother of Ronald M. Randall. Along with his brother he enlisted on June 5, 1861, at Union City and, like his brother, saw action at Belmont. Private Calvin Randall was mortally wounded on April 6, 1862, at the Battle of Shiloh, where his brother removed him from the field. This gallant Southern Illinoisan died in the Confederate hospital at Lauderdale Springs, Mississippi, on May 22 of that same year.

79. **Randall, Private Ronald M.** State of birth: Kentucky. Date of birth: January 2, 1836. State of residency, 1861: Illinois (Marion, Williamson County). Occupation: wagon maker. Description: 5 feet 6 inches, black hair, dark eyes, dark complexion. Ronald M. Randall was the brother of Calvin Randall. Both enlisted at Union City together on June 5, 1861, and both saw action together at Belmont. The gallant Private R. M. Randall temporarily saved his younger brother's life at Shiloh by removing him from the battlefield in spite of being wounded himself. Because of his wounds and illness, he did not re-enlist after one year and was discharged at Tupelo on July 20, 1862.

80. **Roland, Private J. T.** State of birth: Virginia. State of residency, 1861: Illinois (Carbondale, Jackson County). His enlistment took place at Union City on June 5, 1861. He was then engaged at Belmont. At Shiloh on April 6, 1862, the gallant Private J. T. Roland assisted in the

saving of the Fifteenth Tennessee regimental colors. While posted with Sergeant Frank Metcalf's improvised color-guard detachment, this heroic member of G Company was mortally wounded by a shell fragment. The Southern Illinoisan died at Lauderdale Springs on May 29, 1862.

81. **Saunders, Sergeant John T.** State of birth: Tennessee. State of residency, 1861: Kentucky (Mayfield, Graves County). After enlisting on June 5, 1861, at Union City, he was elected as a sergeant for G Company at Island Number Ten on August 19 before being engaged at the November 7 Battle of Belmont. Sergeant Saunders was on unspecified special duty from January 1 to May 1, 1862. He did not re-enlist after his one year term expired and was subsequently discharged from the army on July 20, 1862, at Tupelo.

82. **Sayers, Corporal W. M.** State of birth: Missouri. State of residency, 1861: Kentucky (Paducah, McCracken County). His enlistment took place at Union City on June 5, 1861. He was then engaged at both Belmont and Shiloh. During the reorganization of G Company at Corinth on May 15, 1862, Private W. M. Sayers was elected as a corporal. He deserted at Tupelo in July of that same year.

83. **Sherman, Private Gardner.** State of birth: Indiana (Jefferson County). Date of birth: September 11, 1822. State of residency, 1861: Illinois (Marion, Williamson County). Occupation: farmer. Description: 5 feet 4 inches, dark complexion, black eyes, dark hair. Gardner Sherman was one of the six members of the Southern Illinois Company to have been born and raised in the North. Enlisting June 5, 1861, at Union City he became a combat participant at Belmont and Shiloh. Private Sherman did not re-enlist after his one year hitch and was discharged at Tupelo on July 20, 1862.

84. **Sherty, Private Horace.** State of birth: North Carolina. State of residency, 1861: Tennessee (Coffee County). Occupation: farmer. Description: 5 feet 4 inches, fair complexion, sandy hair, blue eyes. Having enlisted June 5, 1861, at Union City, he was then listed as present for duty at Belmont. On detail with the baggage from January 1 to May 1, 1862, Private Sherty did not re-enlist after his initial tour. At Tupelo on July 20 he was discharged.

85. **Shields, Private David.** State of birth: Tennessee (Clarksville, Montgomery County). State of residency, 1861: Kentucky (Paducah,

McCracken County). He enlisted at Union City on June 5, 1861. The son of Irish immigrants (Gus and Clare) and possibly the only Catholic member of G Company, Private Shields resigned for personal family reasons at Columbus on November 1 of that same year.

86. **Stewart, Private Alfred.** State of birth: Missouri. State of residency, 1861: Kentucky (Paducah, McCracken County). This Western Kentuckian enlisted at Union City on June 5, 1861. After having been engaged at Belmont, he was listed as present for duty at Shiloh. Private Stewart deserted at Corinth on May 20, 1862.

87. **Summerville, Private J. M.** State of birth: Tennessee. State of residency, 1861: Kentucky (Paducah, McCracken County). Enlisting on June 5, 1861, at Union City, Private Summerville was listed as present at Belmont. He ran to the rear in panic at Shiloh on April 6, 1862, and deserted at Corinth on May 20.

88. **Tinker, Private W. R.** State of birth: Tennessee. State of residency, 1861: Illinois (Marion, Williamson County). Following his enlistment on June 5, 1861, at Union City the Southern Illinoisan was engaged at Belmont and Shiloh. Private Tinker did not re-enlist after one year and was discharged from the army at Tupelo on July 20, 1862.

89. **Walker, Private R. L.** State of birth: Kentucky. State of residency, 1861: Illinois (Marion, Williamson County). He registered at Union City on June 5, 1861. After spending time on sick leave from August 16 until October 31, this Southern Illinoisan fought at Belmont, November 7. Seriously wounded on April 6, 1862, at Shiloh the gallant Private Walker was on leave because of his wounds for the remainder of that year. He was declared disabled by the Medical Review Board and discharged on January 1, 1863.

90. **Wall, Major John M.** State of birth: Virginia. Date of birth: September 19, 1832. State of residency, 1861: Kentucky (Mayfield, Graves County). Occupation: medical doctor. Marital status: married, four children. Ancestry: Scotch-Irish. Religion: Presbyterian. Dr. John M. Wall was one of the most courageous and versatile unsung heroes of the Confederacy. He served as company surgeon, company combat officer, regimental assistant surgeon, regimental surgeon, regimental staff officer, and regimental commanding officer. After registering with the other men of Captain Thorndike Brooks' command at Union City on June 5, 1861,

Dr. Wall was appointed as surgeon of the Southern Illinois Company and as an assistant surgeon of the Fifteenth Tennessee Infantry with the commission of first lieutenant. Even though technically a noncombatant, Lieutenant Wall volunteered to fight with the G Company enlisted men at Belmont, Missouri on November 7, 1861, where for the first time he performed his dual role as soldier and doctor. On January 7, 1862, he was appointed Chief Surgeon of the Fifteenth by Lieutenant Colonel Robert C. Tyler with the unofficial rank of brevet captain. On the bloody first morning (April 6, 1862) of the Battle of Shiloh, the gallant Western Kentuckian was given the high risk assignment as Tyler's aide-de-camp on the field, and then risked his life again by remaining on that battlefield to assist the wounded while the shooting continued and the regiment withdrew. Later that same chaotic morning, he provided medical assistance to both Brigadier General Bushrod R. Johnson and Tyler, a future Confederate general. If Wall had been on the other side at Shiloh, he may well have eventually received the coveted United States Medal of Honor. Certainly the doctor had earned the tremendous respect of the men he served with. As a result, a rare honor was bestowed on him at the reorganization of the regiment at Corinth, Mississippi on May 11, 1862. Although commissioned at first only as an army doctor, Brevet Captain Wall was elected to the rank of major, the third-in-command of the Fifteenth Tennessee under Colonel Tyler and Lieutenant Colonel Brooks. He was a combat officer from that moment on, but never completely relinquished his other duties as a staff surgeon. With Tyler recovering from his Shiloh wound, Brooks and Wall, both original members of G Company, became the two ranking officers of the regiment. Major Wall distinguished himself as commander of a battalion (four companies of the Fifteenth) at Perryville on October 8, 1862, playing a key role in the successful attack on the Second Ohio Infantry to gain possession of the Widow Gibson's Farm. Seriously wounded by a Federal sharpshooter outside of Murfreesboro on the last day of that year, the major spent the next six months in various Confederate military hospitals in the Atlanta area. Recuperated from his wounds, he returned to the active roster at the same time that Brooks, also wounded at Murfreesboro, had to go back on sick leave because of his wounds. As a result of this the doctor-soldier commanded the remnant of the Fifteenth Tennessee at the September 19–

20, 1863, Battle of Chickamauga, where he again rotated his dual duties as combat officer and surgeon. When Colonel Robert Dudley Fraser of the Fifteenth/Thirty-Seventh Tennessee fell at Missionary Ridge on November 25 of that same year, Major Wall took command of the consolidated regiment and aided Brigadier General William B. Bate's valiant stand on the crest. Wall and the men of the wounded Colonel Tyler's brigade (Bate's division) were the last Confederates to be forced off the ridge. At the July 22, 1864, Battle of Atlanta, this Southern patriot fought with desperation but was mortally wounded and left on the battlefield, where he died two days later within a few hundred yards from the tent of Union Captain Hibert A. Cunningham. The military record of Major John M. Wall within G Company of the Fifteenth Tennessee is surpassed by none.

91. **Wallace, Private Leroy.** State of birth: Kentucky. State of residency, 1861: Missouri. Personally recruited by Captain Brooks, he enlisted for G Company on August 1, 1861, at New Madrid, Missouri. Private Leroy Wallace, the only Missouri resident of the unit, served exclusively as a noncombatant, attached first to the company and then to the regimental Noncommissioned Officers Staff. He deserted at Chattanooga on September 12, 1863.

92. **Wallace, Private William.** State of birth: Maryland. State of residency, 1861: Illinois (Marion, Williamson County). Private William Wallace enlisted on June 5, 1861, at Union City but then resigned for personal reasons at Columbus on September 15 of that year.

93. **Walston, Corporal B. L.** State of birth: Missouri (Wayne County). Date of birth: October 22, 1844. State of residency, 1861: Tennessee (Nashville, Davidson County). Occupation: farmer. Description: 5 feet, dark complexion, dark eyes, dark hair. One of the two underage members of G Company he enlisted on September 1, 1861, at Island Number Ten before seeing action at both Belmont and Shiloh. This tiny youngster was then elected as a corporal for the company during the reorganization in Corinth on May 15, 1862. Corporal Walston was discharged at Tupelo on July 20 of that year by reason of article eight of the Conscription Act (under age).

94. **Wandell, Sergeant G. W.** State of birth: Arkansas. State of residency, 1861: Illinois (Marion, Williamson County). He enlisted on June 5, 1861, at Union City. Shortly after the organization of the Southern Illinois

Company this Southern Illinoisan was elected as a sergeant. Absent with leave from August 16, 1861, to May 2, 1862, Sergeant Wandell was never engaged in battle, did not re-enlist, and was discharged from the army on July 20, 1862, at Tupelo.

95. **Wheatley, Private R. L.** State of birth: Georgia. State of residency, 1861: Kentucky (Paducah, McCracken County). His enlistment took place at Union City on June 5, 1861. The reliable Private Wheatley participated in all three major battles of G Company, that is, Belmont, Shiloh, and Perryville. He became one of the eight members of the company to be permanently transferred to other assignments or units when he was sent to Cobb's Battery at Murfreesboro in December of 1862.

96. **Wilkerson, Private A. J.** State of birth: Tennessee. State of residency, 1861: Illinois (Marion, Williamson County). After registering on June 5, 1861, at Union City, he was listed as present at Belmont. On April 3, 1862, three days prior to the fighting at Shiloh, Private Wilkerson deserted at Corinth.

97. **Williams, Private M. V.** State of birth: Kentucky. Date of birth: June 30, 1844. State of residency, 1861: Illinois (Carbondale, Jackson County). Occupation: farmer. Description: 5 feet 3 inches, dark complexion, black eyes, dark hair. After his enlistment at Union City on June 5, 1861, he was engaged at the Battle of Belmont on November 7 of that same year. This youthful Southern Illinoisan, as a member of Sergeant Frank Metcalf's improvised detachment, helped salvage the Fifteenth Tennessee color-guard at Shiloh, April 6, 1862. One of two underage members of G Company, the gallant youngster was discharged from the army at Tupelo on July 20 of that same year by reason of article eight of the Conscription Act (under age).

98. **Witt, Private J. K. P.** State of birth: Alabama. State of residency, 1861: Illinois (Marion, Williamson County). His enlistment with the Southern Illinois Company took place on June 5, 1861, at Union City. He was then placed on sick leave between November 1, 1861, and May 1, 1862. Attached to the Fifteenth Tennessee Noncommissioned Officers Staff, June 1, 1862, to February 1, 1864, Private Witt was reactivated to regular duty in the spring and was captured on June 27, 1864, at Kennesaw Mountain. This Southern Illinoisan spent the last months of the war at Camp Chase in Columbus, Ohio before being released at the end.

99. **Wortham, Private E. J. J.** State of birth: Tennessee. State of residency, 1861: Illinois (Marion, Williamson County). He enlisted at Union City on June 5, 1861. Attached to Captain Valentine's Cavalry Company on October 11 of that year, Private Wortham was one of the eight members of G company to be permanently transferred to other assignments or units.

Appendix B

Stastical Data
Compiled Military Service Records,
G Company, Fifteenth Tennessee Infantry

(All officers and men are listed with their highest rank achieved)

Men who enlisted on June 5, 1861, at Union City, Tennessee from Marion, Williamson County, Illinois. Total = 28.

3. Pvt. James Bell	58. Pvt. Alex McKensie
6. Lt. Col. Thorndike Brooks	59. Pvt. A. R. McKinelley
7. Pvt. W. J. Brown	70. Pvt. G.L. Patterson
14. Capt. Hibert A. Cunningham	76. Cpl. G. W. Perry
16. Pvt. W. J. Davis	78. Pvt. Calvin Randall
19. Sgt. G. H. Dodson	79. Pvt. Ronald M. Randall
23. Pvt. John Finnegan	83. Pvt. Gardner Sherman
24. Pvt. Henry Gifford	88. Pvt. W. R. Tinker
34. 2nd Lt. Harvey L. Hays	89. Pvt. R. L. Walker
39. 1st Lt. Henry C. Hopper	92. Pvt. William Wallace
44. Pvt. Flemming Jent	94. Sgt. G. W. Wandell
47. Sgt. Robert R. Kelly	96. Pvt. A. J. Wilkerson
50. Pvt. J. C. Kyle	98. Pvt. J. K. P. Witt
52. Pvt. A. J. Lowe	99. Pvt. E. J. J. Wortham

Men who enlisted on June 5, 1861, at Union City from Carbondale, Jackson County, Illinois. Total = 6.

5. Pvt. Spince Blankenship	60. Sgt. Frank Metcalf
11. Sgt. P. Timothy Corder, Jr.	80. Pvt. J. T. Roland
12. Cpl. P. Timothy Corder, Sr.	97. Pvt. M. V. Williams

Men who enlisted on June 5, 1861, at Union City from Paducah, McCracken County, Kentucky. Total = 21.

1. Pvt. Jeremiah Ables
9. Pvt. J. M. Childers
13. Cpl. Samuel Cree
20. Pvt. B. A. Dudley
21. Cpl. E. Y. Eaker
33. Pvt. G. W. Harrington
35. Pvt. J. T. Hayes
38. Pvt. Titus Holmes
43. Pvt. Fred A. Jenkins
48. Pvt. Calvin R. Klein
55. Pvt. John Mason
56. Sgt. John McClartney
61. Sgt. W. J. Meyer
66. Pvt. Robert Mullens
68. Pvt. J. F. Parkhill
72. Pvt. John Patterson
74. Pvt. F. A. Pentecost
82. Cpl. W. M. Sayers
85. Pvt. David Shields
86. Pvt. Alfred Stewart
95. Pvt. R. L.Wheatley

Men who enlisted on June 5, 1861, at Union City from Mayfield, Graves County, Kentucky. Total = 9.

4. Pvt. J. M. Betts
18. Pvt. A. J. Dillard
26. Pvt. J. D. Goodridge
27. Pvt. Thomas Gowins
46. Pvt. S. T. Jones
63. Pvt. A. H. Morgan
81. Sgt. John T. Saunders
87. Pvt. J. M. Summerville
90. Maj. John M. Wall

Men who enlisted on June 5, 1861, at Union City from Middle Tennessee. Total = 11.

15. Pvt. William Cyerpit
17. Pvt. W. M. Davis
22. Pvt. Calvin H. Ferrell
25. Pvt. Edward Gomand
29. Pvt. John Gray
30. Pvt. Lester Grayham
36. Pvt. W. W. Haywood
54. Pvt. Richard Lyle
62. Pvt. Isreal Moore
67. Pvt. Frank Ogle
84. Pvt. Horace Sherty

Men who enlisted on June 5, 1861, at Union City from Pennsylvania. Total = 2.

2. Pvt. W. L. Baldwin
71. Pvt. J. G. Patterson

Men who enlisted on June 5, 1861, at Union City for A Company from Middle and East Tennessee and were then transferred to G Company on June 6 at Jackson, Tennessee. Total = 9.

10. Pvt. W. J. Cooper (Knoxville)   51. Pvt. J. W. Lewelling
40. 2nd Lt. Bryant W. Hudgens   64. Pvt. Asa G. Morris
42. Pvt. J. A. Hunter   69. Pvt. Joseph Parton
45. Pvt. Joshua B. Johnson   77. Pvt. J. P. Price (Knoxville)
49. Pvt. Daniel Knight

Man who enlisted on June 5, 1861, at Union City from Minnesota.
28. Sgt. Maj. Samuel H. Graham

Man who enlisted on August 1, 1861, at New Madrid, Missouri, from Missouri.
91. Pvt. Leroy Wallace

Men who enlisted at Island No. Ten, Tennessee, from Middle Tennessee. Total = 5.

31. Pvt. J. L. Gryder (Aug. 10)   65. Pvt. James Mowlen (Sept. 1)
37. Pvt. Bryce Holland (Aug. 28)   93. Pvt. B. L. Walston (Sept. 1)
53. Cpl. Joshua Lowe (Aug. 28)

Men who enlisted at Columbus, Kentucky from Mayfield, Graves County, Kentucky. Total = 6.

8. Pvt. C. F. Carmon (Sept. 5)   57. Pvt. D. L. L. McGeehee (Sept.10)
32. Pvt. J. T. Gunn (Sept. 28)   73. Pvt. J. M. Payne (Sept. 30)
41. Pvt. E. C. Hunter (Oct. 8)   75. Pvt. W. T. Pentecost (Sept. 10)

States of Residency, 1861. Total = 99 men.

Kentucky = 36   Pennsylvania = 2
Illinois = 34   Minnesota = 1
Tennessee = 25   Missouri = 1

Places of Birth Known = 96.
Tennessee = 19
Kentucky = 18
Missouri = 13
Virginia = 13
Georgia = 5
Alabama = 4
Maryland = 3
No. Carolina = 3
Ohio = 3
So. Carolina = 3

Unknown = 3.
Arkansas = 2
Indiana = 2
Mississippi = 2
Delaware = 1
Illinois = 1
Louisiana = 1
Texas = 1
Canada = 1
Ireland = 1

Men killed in action. Total = 3.
16. Pvt. W. J. Davis (Shiloh, April 6, 1862)
18. Pvt. A. J. Dillard (Perryville, October 8, 1862)
70. Pvt. G. L. Patterson (Shiloh, April 6, 1862)

Men mortally wounded in action. Total = 8.
8. Pvt. C. F. Carmon (Shiloh, died May 14, 1862)
12. Cpl. P. Timothy Corder, Sr. (Shiloh, died April 13, 1862)
28. Sgt. Maj. Samuel H. Graham (Franklin, died January 12, 1865)
32. Pvt. J. T. Gunn (Shiloh, died April 13, 1862)
65. Pvt. James Mowlen (Shiloh, died April 7, 1862)
78. Pvt. Calvin Randall (Shiloh, died May 22, 1862)
80. Pvt. J. T. Roland (Shiloh, died May 29, 1862)
90. Maj. John M. Wall (Atlanta, died July 24, 1864)

Men disabled by wounds. Total = 11.
5. Pvt. Spince Blankenship (Perryville, Chickamauga, Jonesboro)
23. Pvt. John Finnegan (Perryville)
25. Pvt. Edward Gomand (Jonesboro)
36. Pvt. W. W. Haywood (Shiloh)
41. Pvt. E. C. Hunter (Shiloh)
49. Pvt. Daniel Knight (Shiloh)

60. Sgt. Frank Metcalf (Perryville)
63. Pvt. A. H. Morgan (Belmont)
64. Pvt. Asa G. Morris (Chickamauga)
72. Pvt. John Patterson (Shiloh)
89. Pvt. R. L. Walker (Shiloh)

Men seriously wounded but not disabled. Total = 5.
6. Lt. Col. Thorndike Brooks (First Murfreesboro)
13. Cpl. Samuel Cree (Belmont)
59. Pvt. A. R. McKinelly (Belmont)
79. Pvt. Ronald M. Randall (Shiloh)
90. Maj. John M. Wall (First Murfreesboro, later killed)

Men captured, exchanged, and discharged. Total = 9.
1. Pvt. Jeremiah Ables (First Murfreesboro)
15. Pvt. William Cyerpit (Shiloh)
22. Pvt. Calvin Henderson Ferrell (Shiloh)
26. Pvt. J. D. Goodridge (Shiloh)
29. Pvt. John Gray (Shiloh)
54. Pvt. Richard Lyle (Shiloh)
62. Pvt. Isreal Moore (Shiloh)
67. Pvt. Frank Ogle (Kennesaw Mountain)
98. Pvt. J. K. P. Witt (Kennesaw Mountain)

Men discharged because of illness. Total = 3.
31. Pvt. J. L. Gryder
35. Pvt. J. T. Hayes
48. Pvt. Calvin R. Klein

Men declared unfit by the Medical Review Board and discharged. Total = 6.

4. Pvt. J. M. Betts
9. Pvt. J. M. Childers
50. Pvt. J. C. Kyle
74. Pvt. F. A. Pentecost
93. Pvt. B. L. Walston (underage)
97. Pvt. M. V. Williams (underage)

Men transferred to other assignments or units. Total = 8.

2. Pvt. W. L. Baldwin
20. Pvt. B. A. Dudley
22. Pvt. C. H. Ferrell
45. Pvt. Joshua B. Johnson

61. Sgt. W. J. Meyer
71. Pvt. J. G. Patterson
95. Pvt. R. L.Wheatley
99. Pvt. E. J. J. Wortham

Men who resigned for personal reasons. Total = 5.

30. Pvt. Lester Grayham
39. 1st Lt. Henry C. Hopper
47. Sgt. Robert R. Kelly

85. Pvt. David Shields
92. Pvt. William Wallace

Men who did not re-enlist after one year. Total = 16.

3. Pvt. James Bell
7. Pvt. W. J. Brown
11. Sgt. P. T. Corder, Jr.
17. Pvt. W. M. Davis
53. Cpl. Joshua Lowe
55. Pvt. John Mason
58. Pvt. Alex McKenzie
59. Pvt. A. R. McKinelly

69. Pvt. J. J. Parton
73. Pvt. J. M. Payne
79. Pvt. Ronald M. Randall
81. Sgt. John T. Saunders
83. Pvt. Gardner Sherman
84. Pvt. Horace Sherty
88. Pvt. W. R. Tinker
94. Sgt. G. W. Wandell

Men who made it all the way, Belmont to Bentonville. Total = 3.

6. Lt. Col. Thorndike Brooks
40. 2nd Lt. Bryant W. Hudgens

66. Pvt. Robert Mullens

Men who were cashiered from the army. Total = 2.

27. Pvt. Thomas Gowins

34. 2nd Lt. Harvey L. Hays

Men who went over to the other side. Total = 2.

14. Capt. Hibert A. Cunningham

43. Pvt. Fred A. Jenkins

Men who deserted. Total = 24.

10. Pvt. W. J. Cooper
14. Capt. Hibert A. Cunningham

52. Pvt. A. J. Lowe
56. Sgt. John McClartney

19. Sgt. G. H. Dodson

21. Cpl. E. Y. Eaker

24. Pvt. Henry Gifford

33. Pvt. G. W. Harrington

37. Pvt. Bryce Holland

38. Pvt. Titus Holmes

42. Pvt. J. A. Hunter

44. Pvt. Jent Flemming

46. Pvt. S. T. Jones

51. Pvt. J. W. Lewelling

57. Pvt. D. L. L. McGeehee

68. Pvt. J. F. Parkhill

75. Pvt. W. T. Pentecost

76. Cpl. G. W. Perry

77. Pvt. J. P. Price

82. Cpl. W. M. Sayers

86. Pvt. Alfred Stewart

87. Pvt. J. M. Summerville

91. Pvt. Leroy Wallace

96. Pvt. A. J. Wilkerson

Men who were born and raised in the Free States. Total = 6.

2. Pvt. William L. Baldwin (born in Ohio, resident of Pennsylvania)

5. Pvt. Spince Blankenship (born in Indiana, resident of Illinois)

16. Pvt. W. J. Davis (born in Ohio, resident of Illinois)

47. Sgt. Robert R. Kelly (born in Illinois, resident of Illinois)

71. Pvt. J. G. Patterson (born in Ohio, resident of Pennsylvania)

83. Pvt. Gardner Sherman (born in Indiana, resident of Illinois)

(Sgt. Maj. Samuel H. Graham may well have been a seventh member of this group, but since his place of birth is unknown it cannot be assumed that he was not born in the South.)

Men who ran to the rear in panic at Shiloh. Total = 7.

10. Pvt. J. M. Cooper

24. Pvt. Henry Gifford

46. Pvt. S. T. Jones

52. Pvt. A. J. Lowe

68. Pvt. J. F. Parkhill

77. Pvt. J. P. Price

87. Pvt. J.M. Summerville

The commissioned officers by rank. Total = 6.

6. Lt. Col. Thorndike Brooks of Illinois

90. Maj. John M. Wall of Kentucky

14. Capt. Hibert A. Cunningham of Illinois

39. 1st Lt. Henry C. Hopper of Illinois

35. 2nd Lt. Harvey L. Hays of Illinois

40. 2nd Lt. Bryant W. Hudgens of Tennessee

Southern Illinoisans with distinguished service records. Total = 14.

5. Pvt. Spince Blankenship
6. Lt. Col. Thorndike Brooks
11. Sgt. P. T. Corder, Jr.
12. Cpl. P. T. Corder, Sr.
16. Pvt. W. J. Davis
23. Pvt. John Finnegan
59. Pvt. A. R. McKinelly

60. Sgt. Frank Metcalf
70. Pvt. G. L. Patterson
78. Pvt. Calvin Randall
79. Pvt. Ronald M. Randall
80. Pvt. J. T. Roland
89. Pvt. R. L. Walker
97. Pvt. M. V. Williams

Southern Illinoisans with virtually no service records at all, or service records with mixed positive and negative aspects. Total = 13.

3. Pvt. James Bell
7. Pvt. W. J. Brown
35. 2nd Lt. H. L. Hays
39. 1st Lt. H. C. Hopper
47. Sgt. R. R. Kelly
50. Pvt. J. C. Kyle
58. Pvt. Alex McKensie

83. Pvt. Gardner Sherman
88. Pvt. W. R. Tinker
92. Pvt. William Wallace
94. Sgt. G. W. Wandell
98. Pvt. J. K. P. Witt
99. Pvt. E. J. J. Wortham

Southern Illinoisans with negative service records. Total = 7.

14. Capt. Hibert A. Cunningham
19. Sgt. G. H. Dodson
24. Pvt. Henry Gifford
44. Pvt. Flemming Jent

52. Pvt. A. J. Lowe
76. Cpl. G. W. Perry
96. Pvt. A. J. Wilkerson

Notes

Chapter One
Harry Hopper Secedes From The Union

Information concerning the recruitment and organization of Thorndike Brooks' Southern Illinois squadron comes from seven sources—four from the nineteenth century, three from the twentieth. Two of the nineteenth century sources are those of Sergeant Frank Metcalf—his two letters to Judge J. M. Dickinson and his own article in *Confederate Veteran (CV)*. The other two are Dickinson's article in *CV* and one entry in Milo Erwin's 1876 *History of Williamson County, Illinois*. Richard Weinert's brief modern (1961) article in *Civil War Times Illustrated (CWTI)* is based on these four original sources. Modern Illinois historians Victor Hicken and John Y. Simon offer one paragraph each. All of this is somewhat deceiving, however. Dickinson's article consists mostly of quotes from Metcalf's letters, and Metcalf himself wrote the entry in Erwin. In reality all of the writers—Metcalf, Dickinson, Erwin, Weinert, Hicken, and Simon— knowingly or unknowingly use one and the same eyewitness account— Metcalf's.

It was assumed by many Southern Illinois residents in April of 1861, that pro-Southern volunteer companies would be raised throughout the counties of John A. Logan's Ninth Illinois Congressional District and that the congressman himself would lead a full regiment south. In Congress Logan had consistently been a strong proponent of states rights and slavery. He gave the lasting impression to many of his fellow Democrats that he was about to declare himself for secession and the Southern Confederacy. Logan's young brother-in-law, Hibert A. Cunningham, took a pro-secession stance at least in part because of the congressman's influence. When Logan declared for the Union at the Marion Town Square in August, he took the rest of Egypt with him. (The Eighteenth Illinois Infantry had already been raised in the southern counties.) Those same southern counties supplied the men for Colonel Logan's Thirty-First Illinois Infantry, with an especially heavy representation of men from Williamson County. A number of pro-Confederate Southern Illinoisans, like Frank Metcalf, held a grudge against Logan for what they considered deliberate deception.

Some historians state that the Illinois State Militia troops at Big Muddy Bridge Depot in Jackson County near Murphysboro and Carbondale were sent from Chicago and Peoria by Governor Richard Yates in Springfield, while others maintain that they were sent up from Cairo by Colonel B.M. Prentiss. Both positions are correct. Prentiss' Tenth Illinois Infantry was reinforced by rail from Chicago and Peoria by Yates in Springfield. Some of the reinforcements were used at Big Muddy.

1. Cottingham, Carl D., Preston Michael Jones, and Gary W. Kent. *General John A. Logan: His Life and Times*, p. 1; *Report of the Illinois Adjutant General*, vol. 1, pp. 5–7; Weinert, Richard P., "The Illinois Confederates," *Civil War Times Illustrated (CWTI)*, vol. 2, p. 44.

2. Erwin, Milo. "Williamson County, Illinois: Historical Essays," Illinois State Historical Library, Springfield, p. 99; Smith, George W. *A History of Southern Illinois*, vol. 1, introduction.

3. Morris, W. S., L. D. Hartwell, and J. B. Kuykendall. *History: Thirty-First Regiment Illinois Volunteers*, Forward by John Y. Simon, p. IX.

4. Long, E.B. *The Civil War Day By Day: An Almanac, 1861–1865*, p. 64; Warner, Ezra J. *Generals in Blue*, pp. 385–6.

5. Erwin, Milo. *A History of Williamson County, Illinois*, p. 257.

6. Dickinson, J. M., "Secession Spirit (1861) In Illinois," *Confederate Veteran (CV)*, vol. 9, p. 5.

7. Metcalf, Frank. September 29, 1900 letter to Judge J. M. Dickinson.

8. *Chicago Daily Tribune*, April 19, 1861.

9. Erwin, *Williamson County*, p. 257.

10. Dickinson, "Secession Spirit," *CV*, vol. 9, p. 5.

11. Hicken, Victor. *Illinois in the Civil War*, p. 13; Metcalf, Frank, "The Illinois Confederate Company," *CV*, vol. 16, p. 224.

12. Erwin, *Williamson County*, p. 257.

13. *Cairo Argus*, April 29, 1861; Erwin, "Historical Essays," p. 99; Simon, John Y. "Civil War Comes to Williamson County,"

Springhouse, vol. 8, no. 6, p. 34.

14. Dickinson, "Secession Spirit," *CV*, vol. 9, pp. 5–6.
15. Metcalf, September 29, 1900 letter to Dickinson.
16. Confederate Service Records (CSR), Tennessee State Library and Archives (TSLA).
17. Metcalf, September 29, 1900 letter to Dickinson.
18. CSR, TSLA.
19. Dickinson, "Secession Spirit," *CV*, vol. 9, p. 6.
20. Erwin, *Williamson County*, p. 257.
21. Metcalf, "Illinois Confederate Company," *CV*, vol. 16, p. 225.
22. Ibid.
23. Weinert, "Illinois Confederates," *CWTI*, vol. 2, p. 44.
24. CSR, TSLA.
25. Metcalf, September 29, 1900 letter to Dickinson.
26. CSR, TSLA.
27. Metcalf, "Illinois Confederate Company," *CV*, vol. 16, p. 225.

Chapter Two
Harvey Hays Declares War

The strange but true incident at Milburn virtually destroyed the military reputation of the Fifteenth Tennessee Infantry before the first shot was fired. Because of its early resignation and desertion rate, G Company came away from the dreadful march appearing to be the worst company of the worst regiment at Columbus. What was needed, of course, was competent leadership from the regimental field officers and the company line officers.

The rank of lieutenant colonel given to Robert Charles Tyler on October 14, 1861, was "temporary," that is, without the official sanction of the Richmond War Department. The promotion had to take effect immediately so that Major John F. Hearn, the second ranking officer of the regiment, would not rank Tyler, the field commander of the regiment. Tyler's commission became permanent on December 4. At the time of his temporary appointment as lieutenant colonel of the Fifteenth Tennessee, R.C. Tyler was every bit as obscure as the Southern Illinoisans in his new command. Because of his apparent lack of living relatives, much has been suggested about the "mystery" of the young Marylander who drifted to Memphis in 1860, much of which has been clarified by Bruce Allardice's article in the January/February 1995 issue of *CWTI*.

Even Tyler's Confederate military career is hard to keep straight, as the oft-wounded officer was moved back and forth from combat commands to special assignments. After Shiloh the army considered Tyler and the Fifteenth to be a pleasant surprise. In point of fact the "mysterious" colonel and his regiment had been underestimated from the start due to the ridiculous affair on the road from Columbus to Milburn.

1. Allardice, Bruce, February 14, 1995, letter to the author in regards to the Carroll family; Horn, Stanley F., Editor. "Fifteenth Tennessee Infantry Regiment," *Tennesseeans in the Civil War*, vol. 1, pp. 205–6.

2. Carroll, Charles M. "Fifteenth Tennessee Infantry," from *Military Annals of Tennessee: Confederate* by Dr. John B. Lindsley, p. 332; Metcalf, September 29, 1900 letter to Dickinson.

3. CSR, TSLA for W.L. Baldwin, T. Brooks, S.H. Graham, J. G. Patterson; Muster Roll, "Fifteenth Tennessee Infantry," National Archives and Records Administration (NARA), Confederate Record Group (RG) No. 109, September 1, 1861.

4. CSR, TSLA for T. Brooks, C.M. Carroll, H.A. Cunningham, H. L. Hays, H. C. Hopper, R. R. Kelly, F. Metcalf, J. M. Wall.

5. CSR, TSLA.

6. Metcalf, "Illinois Confederate Company," *CV*, vol. 16, p. 225.

7. Muster Roll (NARA), RG No. 109, September 1, 1861.

8. CSR, TSLA for B.G. Ezzell; Metcalf, September 29, 1900 letter to Dickinson.

9. CSR, TSLA.

10. Horn, "Fifteenth Tennessee," vol. 1, p. 206.

11. Carroll, "Fifteenth Tennessee," (Lindsley), p. 333.

12. CSR, TSLA.

13. Cottingham, *Logan*, p. 11; Porter, George C., "Tennessee Confederate Regiments: The Fifteenth," Document No. 39, TSLA; Simon. "Civil War Comes to Williamson County," *Springhouse*,

vol. 8, no. 6, p. 34.

14. CSR, TSLA.

15. Ibid.

16. Ibid for S. H. Graham, R. R. Kelly.

17. Force, M.F. *From Fort Henry to Corinth*, pp. 7-10; Walke, Henry, "The Gunboats At Belmont and Fort Henry," *Battles and Leaders of the Civil War (BL)*, vol. 1, pp. 360–1.

18. Polk, William M., "General Polk and the Battle of Belmont," *BL*, vol. 1, p. 348.

19. Grant, U.S. *Personal Memoirs*, vol. 1, p. 261; Monogham, Jay. *Swamp Fox of the Confederacy*, pp. 30–40; Morris, *Thirty-First Illinois*, p. 18.

20. Army Official Records (AOR), Serial No. 3, p. 343 (Cheatham).

21. Simon, John Y. *Papers of U. S. Grant*, vol. 3, pp. 121–2.

22. *St. Louis Sunday Republican*, November 10, 1861.

23. CSR, TSLA for C. M. Carroll, J. F. Hearn.

24. Metcalf, September 29, 1900, letter to Dickinson.

25. Ibid.

26. Army of Tennessee Inspection Report, November 1, 1861, NARA, RG No. 109. (Confederate Western army inspection reports for this period are listed under "Army of Tennessee" even though this army was not formally organized until 1863.)

27. Ibid; AOR, Serial No. 3, p. 296 (Lauman).

28. CSR, TSLA for J. F. Hearn.

29. Allardice, Bruce. "Out of the Shadows," *CWTI*, Jan./Feb. 1995, pp. 27–9; Davis, William C., Editor. *Confederate General*, vol. 6, p. 67; Warner, Ezra J. *Generals in Gray*, p. 313.

Chapter Three
Baptism at Belmont

The overall performance of the Fifteenth Tennessee at the Battle of Belmont, Missouri was poor because of the fact that six of the ten companies broke and ran after the first volley was fired at them. The overall performance of G Company, one of the units that held its position to the north of the Thirty-First Illinois, was good but not above the ordinary. If nothing else, Captain Brooks and his men demonstrated their ability to hold up under fire and to keep up with the columns of advancing infantry. The disintegration of the Fifteenth in battle was precisely what General Polk had feared after the Milburn incident. Part of the problem was the lack of leadership within the internal structure of the companies. Another part was the inexperience of acting Lieutenant Colonel Tyler in regards to field command. Appropriately two of the companies which had done some of the brawling on the Milburn march, the Washington Rifles and G Company, had also done a commendable job of fighting the enemy. The stable performance of the Southern Illinois Company was, in fact, better than what had been expected by Generals Polk, Pillow, and Cheatham.

The Confederate Military Service Records (CSR) of the individual members of G company provide few facts about deployment details at Belmont. Except for some positive words about Brevet Second Lieutenant Harvey Hays, Sergeant Frank Metcalf adds little. Battlefield positions can, however, be pieced together by combining the reports from both sides in Army Official Records (AOR). The Northern point of view can be seen in the personal memoirs of General U.S. Grant, plus Professor John Y. Simon's papers and articles on the subject of Grant at Belmont. Several nineteenth century essays from the *CV* and the *Southern Historical Society Papers (SHSP)* offer an insight into the Southern point of view. However, General Pillow's lengthy and mostly useless report is more of a dissertation on Southern manhood than a battlefield description.

The best and most complete source about Belmont is Dr. Nat Hughes Jr.'s modern work—*The Battle of Belmont: Grant Strikes South.*

1. Hughes, Nathaniel C., Jr. *The Battle of Belmont: Grant Strikes South,* pp. 50–1.

2. Allardice, Bruce. *More Generals in Gray,* p. 219; Horn, Stanley F. *Army of Tennessee,* p. 64.

3. Dawson, G. F. *Life and Services of General John A. Logan: Soldier and Statesman,* p. 19; Dyer, Frederick H. *Compendium of the War of Rebellion,* "31st Regiment," vol. 3, p. 1059; Navy Official Records (NOR), vol. 22, pp. 399–402.

4. AOR, Serial No. 3, p. 307 (Polk).

5. *New Orleans Daily Crescent*, October 29, 1861.

6. Hughes, *Belmont*, p. 71; Sifakis, Stewart. *Compendium of the Confederate Armies: Florida and Arkansas*, p. 94.

7. AOR, Serial No. 3, p. 350 (Polk); *New Orleans Daily Crescent*, November 13, 1861.

8. Horn, *Tennesseeans in the Civil War*, "Second Tennessee Volunteer Infantry Regiment," vol. 1, p. 174; *Memphis Daily Appeal*, November 9, 10, 1861; Morris, W. S. *Thirty-First Illinois*, p. 24.

9. Hicken, *Illinois in the Civil War*, p. 21; Metcalf, October 22, 1900 letter to J. M. Dickinson.

10. AOR, Serial No. 3, p. 354 (Marks) and p. 336 (Tyler).

11. Ibid, p. 359 (Beltzhoover); Metcalf, October 22, 1900 letter to Dickinson.

12. *Daily Missouri Republican*, January 16, 1886.

13. *Memphis Daily Appeal*, November 12, 1861; Porter, James D., *Tennessee* (volume of *Confederate Military History*), p. 12.

14. Grant, *Memoirs*, vol. 1, p. 274; Hicken, *Illinois in the Civil War*, p. 20.

15. Bell, Tyree H. "Report of the Battle of Belmont," Morris Library, Southern Illinois University (SIU); Carnes, W. W., "In the Battle of Belmont," *CV*, vol. 39, p. 369.

16. AOR, Serial No. 3, p. 343 (Cheatham); Cottingham, *General John A. Logan*, p. 11; Hubbard, G. H., "In the Battle of Belmont, Mo.," *CV*, vol. 30, p. 459; Porter, George C., Document No. 39, TSLA, "Tennessee Confederate Regiments: The Fifteenth."

17. AOR, Serial No. 3, p. 354 (Marks); Lake, Lewis F., "My War Service as a Member of Taylor's Battery, Company B, First Illinois Light Artillery Battery," Illinois Historical Library (IHL), Springfield.

18. CSR, TSLA for T. Brooks, M. Dwyer, N. Frech, W. B. Isler; *Memphis Daily Appeal*, November 12, 1861; Morris, *Thirty-First Illinois* (Simon's introduction), p. XI; Singletary, Don, "The Battle of Belmont," *CV*, vol. 23, p. 507.

19. AOR, Serial No. 3, p. 355 (Marks); Metcalf, October 22, 1900,

letter to Dickinson; Schwartz, Adolphus, "The Battle of Belmont," Chicago Historical Society (CHS).

20. Hughes, *Belmont*, pp. 145–6; *New Orleans Daily Crescent*, November 11, 1861.

21. Horn, *Tennesseeans in the Civil War*, "154th (Senior) Tennessee Infantry Regiment," vol. 1, p. 309; Simon, John Y., "Grant At Belmont," *Military Affairs Magazine (MA)*, vol. 45, p. 165.

22. AOR, Serial No. 3, p. 288 (Logan) and p. 344 (Cheatham); Dawson, *Life and Services of Logan*, p. 20; Johnson, Timothy D., "Benjamin Franklin Cheatham at Belmont," *Missouri Historical Review (MHR)*, vol. 81, p. 167; Kurtz, Henry I., "The Battle of Belmont," *CWTI*, vol. 3, p. 23; Morris, *Thirty-First Illinois*, p. 26.

23. CSR, TSLA for F. A. Jenkins.

24. Metcalf, October 22, 1900 letter to Dickinson; *Nashville Banner*, November 13, 1861; Wright, Marcus Joseph, "The Battle of Belmont," *SHSP*, vol. 16, p. 80.

25. AOR, Serial No. 3, p. 289 (Logan) and p. 299 (Lauman); Barnwell, Robert W., "The Battle of Belmont," *CV*, vol. 39, p. 371; Metcalf, October 22, 1900 letter to Dickinson.

26. Polk, William M., "General Polk and the Battle of Belmont," *BL*, vol. 1, p. 355; Simon, "Grant at Belmont," *MA*, vol. 45, p. 166.

27. *Chicago Daily Tribune*, November 9, 1861; CSR, TSLA for S. Cree, A. R. McKinelly, A. H. Morgan; Hughes, *Belmont*, pp. 184–5.

28. Horn, *Tennesseeans in the Civil War*, "Fifteenth Tennessee Infantry Regiment," vol. 1, p. 206.

29. Losson, Christopher. *Tennessee's Forgotten Warriors: Frank Cheatham and His Confederate Division*, p. 44; Warner, Ezra J., *Generals in Gray*, p. 283.

30. Connelly, Thomas Lawrence. *Army of the Heartland: Army of Tennessee 1861–1862*, pp. 145–57.

31. Dawson, G. F., *Life and Services of Logan* (introduction); Metcalf, October 22, 1900, letter to Dickinson; Warner, *Generals in Blue*, p. 282.

Chapter Four
Twelve Minutes of Fame at Shiloh

On the morning of the first day at Shiloh—Sunday, April 6, 1862—Colonel Joseph Cockerill of the Seventieth Ohio Infantry looked at his pocket watch. The enemy command in his front, in spite of facing a crossfire of canister and musketry, held its partly exposed position for exactly twelve minutes. Cockerill had no way of knowing that the enemy force was, in fact, a single regiment, namely the Fifteenth Tennessee Infantry. Those twelve minutes represented the shining moment of glory for the obscure Southern regiment. Those same twelve minutes essentially ended the history of G Company as a separate and viable combat unit.

Following the Federal artillery barrage and after both R. C. Tyler and B. R. Johnson fell, T. Brooks withdrew the infantry along with the gunners and guns of Captain M. T. Polk's battery. It was at this time that all six Jackson County, Illinois, members of G Company helped rescue the colors and rally the color-guard. This was not a historical coincidence. The six Carbondale men were close friends and spent most of their time together, on and off the battlefield. Two of the six, F. Metcalf and S. Blankenship, later repeated their color-guard heroics at Perryville.

Within AOR the reports of Confederate Generals Cheatham and Johnson taken together with the reports of Union Colonels Buckland and Cockerill establish the movements and positions of the Fifteenth Tennessee on the Confederate left, Union right. The most detailed modern source for the events in that particular sector of the battlefield is Wiley Sword's award-winning 1974 work, *Shiloh: Bloody April.*

Some other modern accounts claim that Major J. F. Hearn took command of the regiment after R. C. Tyler was wounded. This was not the case. B. F. Cheatham was angry and did not file a complete report at that time. In his personal Shiloh papers he clearly stated, however, that Hearn was serving with him at the position assumed by the 154th Senior Tennessee Infantry. Also in later years Cheatham praised the Irish and German troops of his division. He was not, however, referring to the Irish companies of the Second Tennessee or the German companies of the Fifteenth Tennessee. He was, in fact, praising the Irish-Americans and the German-Americans of the 154th Senior Tennessee.

B. R. Johnson gave temporary regimental command to T. Brooks without having any idea who the Southern Illinoisan was. Five weeks later Brooks was identified as the "captain commanding" in the army inspection report. Given that kind of respect for Brooks' leadership qualities, it is not surprising that he was elected as the lieutenant colonel of the Fifteenth at the time of the reorganization.

1. Lindsley, J. B. *Military Annals of Tennessee: Confederate*, Carroll, C.M., "Fifteenth Tennessee Infantry," p. 333; Horn, *Tennesseeans in the Civil War*, "154th (Senior) Tennessee Infantry Regiment," vol. 1, p. 309; Sifakis, Stewart. *Compendium of the Confederate Armies: Tennessee*, "Tennessee Fifteenth Infantry Regiment," p. 115; Warner, *Generals In Gray*, pp. 157–8.

2. Boatner, Mark III, Editor. *Civil War Dictionary*, p. 754.

3. Faust, Patricia L., Editor. *Encyclopedia of the Civil War*, p. 684.

4. Force, M.F. *From Fort Henry to Corinth*, pp. 102–3.

5. Johnston, W.P., "A. S. Johnston at Shiloh," *BL*, vol. 1, p. 550; Metcalf, October 22, 1900, letter to Dickinson.

6. Cummings, Charles M. *Yankee Quaker Confederate General: The Curious Career of Bushrod Rust Johnson*, p. 217; Horn, *Tennesseeans in the Civil War*, "Second Tennessee Volunteer Infantry Regiment," vol. 1, p. 175; Muster Roll, NARA, RG No. 109, April 1, 1862.

7. Foote, Shelby. *The Civil War: A Narrative, Fort Sumter to Perryville*, p. 331; McDonough, James Lee. *Shiloh—In Hell Before Night*, p. 100.

8. AOR, Serial No. 11, p. 248 (Sherman); Mason, George, "Shiloh," *Sketches of War History, 1861-1865, Military Order of the Loyal Legion of the United States, Ohio Commandery*, vol. 1, pp. 98–101.

9. AOR, Serial No. 11, p. 266 (Buckland); Dyer, *Compendium*, vol. 3, p. 1035, p. 1529; Eddy, Thomas M. *The Patriotism of Illinois*, vol. 1, pp. 320–1; Nicolay, J. G. and John Hay. *Abraham Lincoln: A History*, vol. 5, p. 325.

10. AOR, Serial No. 11, p. 264 (Hildebrand); Dyer, *Compendium*, vol. 3, p. 1521; Hicken, *Illinois in the Civil War*, p. 56.

11. AOR, Serial No. 11, p. 580 (Cleburne); Sword, Wiley. *Shiloh: Bloody April*, p. 201.

12. AOR, Serial No. 11, pp. 437–8 (Cheatham); Ruggles, Daniel,

"Notes on the Shiloh Campaign," *SHSP*, vol. 9, pp. 49–52; Steele, Matthew F. *American Campaigns*, p. 176.

13. Sandridge, L. D. "Battle of Shiloh," *SHSP*, vol. 8, pp. 174–5.

14. AOR, Serial No. 11, p. 445 (B. R. Johnson); Johnson, B. R., "Shiloh," Manuscripts Division, Library of Congress (L of C).

15. Cummings, *Bushrod Johnson*, p. 218; Porter, George C. "Tennessee Confederate Regiments: The Fifteenth," Document No. 39, TSLA; Porter, James D., *Tennessee*, p. 34; Sword, *Shiloh*, p. 206.

16. AOR, Serial No. 11, p. 442 (Cheatham) and pp. 444–5 (B. R. Johnson); CSR, TSLA for J. F. Hearn, M. T. Polk, R. C. Tyler and J. M. Wall; Metcalf, October 22, 1900, letter to Dickinson.

17. AOR, Serial No. 11, p. 271 (Cockerill); Johnson, B.R., "Shiloh," Manuscripts Division, L of C.

18. AOR, Serial No. 11, pp. 275–6 (Barrett); Metcalf, October 22, 1900, letter to Dickinson.

19. CSR, TSLA for J. M. Cooper, H. Gifford, S. T. Jones, A. J. Lowe, J. F. Parkhill, J. P. Price, J. M. Summerville.

20. Bearss, Edwin C. "Artillery Study," Shiloh Military National Park Library; CSR, TSLA for W. W. Haywood, C. Randall, R. M. Randall.

21. CSR, TSLA for S. Blankenship, P. T. Corder, Sr., P. T. Corder, Jr., F. Metcalf, J. T. Roland, M. V. Williams; Horn, *Tennesseeans in the Civil War*, "Captain Marshall T. Polk's Tennessee Light Artillery Company," vol. 1, p. 144; Metcalf, October 22, 1900 letter to Dickinson.

22. AOR, Serial No. 11, p. 250 (Sherman), p. 440 (Cheatham), and p. 445 (B. R. Johnson).

23. Horn, *Tennesseeans in the Civil War*, "Fifteenth Tennessee Infantry Regiment," vol. 1, p. 206; Lindsley, *Military Annals of Tennessee: Confederate*, Carroll, "Fifteenth Tennessee Infantry," pp. 334–5; Livermore, Thomas. *Numbers and Losses in the Civil War*, pp. 79–80; Muster Roll, NARA, RG No. 109, May 15, 1862.

24. CSR, TSLA for C. F. Carmon, P. T. Corder, Sr., W. J. Davis, J. T. Gunn, J. Mowlen, G. L. Patterson, C. Randall, J. T. Roland.

25. AOR, Serial No. 11, pp. 250–4 (Sherman); McDonough, *Shiloh*, p. 116.

26. AOR, Serial No. 11, pp. 384–5 (Beauregard); Dosch, Donald F., "The Hornets Nest," Shiloh Military National Park Library; Jordan, Thomas, "Notes of a Confederate Staff Officer at Shiloh," *BL*, vol. 1, pp. 600-601; Smith, Clifton H., "Letter to General P.G.T. Beauregard: August 5, 1880," CHS.

27. Chisolm, A. R. "The Shiloh Battle Order," *BL*, vol. 1, p. 606; Derry, J. T., "Battle of Shiloh," *SHSP*, vol. 29, pp. 357–60; Grant, U.S., "The Battle of Shiloh," *BL*, vol. 1, pp. 476–86; Kay, William, "The Sunken Road," Shiloh Military National Park Library.

28. CSR, TSLA for T. Brooks, C. M. Carroll, J. F. Hearn, F. Metcalf, R. C. Tyler, J. M. Wall; Horn, *Tennesseeans in the Civil War*, "Fifteenth Tennessee Infantry Regiment," vol. 1, p. 206.

29. Army of Tennessee Inspection Report, May 15, 1862, RG No. 109, NARA; CSR, TSLA for H. A. Cunningham, S. H. Graham, H. L. Hays, H. C. Hopper; Horn, *Tennesseeans in the Civil War*, "Fifteenth Tennessee Infantry Regiment, vol. 1, pp. 206–7; Lindsley, *Military Annals of Tennessee: Confederate*, Carroll, "Fifteenth Tennessee Infantry," p. 333.

30. CSR, TSLA for H.A. Cunningham, H. L. Hayes, H. C. Hopper, B. W. Hudgens.

31. Ibid., for T. Brooks. H. A. Cunningham, H. L. Hays, H. C. Hopper, B. W. Hudgens, J. M. Wall.

32. Ibid., for B. L. Walston, M. V. Williams; Muster Roll, RG No. 109, NARA, August 15, 1862.

33. Porter, George C., "Tennessee Confederate Regiments: The Fifteenth," Document No. 39, TSLA.

34. CSR, TSLA for J. Ables, S. Blankenship, A. S. Dillard, J. Finnegan, E. Gomand, S. H. Graham, F. Metcalf, A. G. Morris, R. Mullens, F. Ogle.

35. Muster Roll, RG No. 109, NARA, August 15, 1862.

Chapter Five
Glory at Gibson's Farm: Perryville

Kenneth A. Hofendorfer's 1981 book, *Perryville: Battle for Kentucky*, provides the most comprehensive account ever written about the strange struggle. Hofendorfer, however, committed a minor error of omission that can be confusing to readers interested in the history of the Fifteenth Tennessee. Throughout the outstanding work he identifies the Fifteenth as "Tyler's regiment" which, although technically correct, fails to mention the name of the actual commanding officer on the field, leaving the reader with the false impression that Colonel Tyler himself was in command of his own small regiment *only* on October 8, 1862. Tyler was, in fact, commanding a "demi-brigade," that is, about half of General D.S. Donelson's brigade. According to army inspection reports and the Confederate Military Service Records (CSR) for both Tyler and Brooks, Tyler was serving as a divisional staff officer that afternoon while Brooks commanded the remnant of the Fifteenth. At dusk Donelson's regiments and Tyler's regiments were reunited. During the final assault of General Cheatham's division, Tyler took command of the brigade's front line and performed extremely well. By late in the day the gallant old Donelson was described as "exhausted." Some of the exhaustion was due to heavy drinking. Cheatham probably drank as much as Donelson that day but was nearly twenty years younger and in better physical condition.

Except for Belmont and the first few minutes at Shiloh, Lieutenant Colonel Brooks commanded the undersized Fifteenth through most of the war, with Tyler commanding larger troop detachments as time passed. After Shiloh, Tyler served first as a staff officer, as Army of Tennessee Provost Marshall, and then as a brigade commander. For the past 130 years the Fifteenth Tennessee Infantry has been remembered as "Tyler's regiment." In reality it was "Brooks' regiment." General Robert Charles Tyler will always be better remembered as the commanding officer of the five regiments that proudly bore the name "Tyler's Brigade" long after the general had been disabled. The regiments of Tyler's brigade of General William B. Bate's division were the Thirty-Seventh Georgia, the Tenth Tennessee, the Fifteenth/Thirty-Seventh Tennessee, the Twentieth Tennessee, and the Thirtieth Tennessee. The author's first book, *Rebel Sons of*

Erin, is a unit history of the Irish Tenth Tennessee. Materials related to Tyler's brigade are listed in the bibliography of this book.

For deployment purposes at Perryville, Brooks divided his regiment into two small but viable battalions. As was the case until the day he died, Major John M. Wall handled his men remarkably well in combat. His command of four companies of about 150 men reinforced the Thirty-Eighth Tennessee in an effective offensive movement against the Second Ohio Infantry. Wall's battalion advanced with the front line of Donelson's detachment throughout the action. On the other hand, the performance of Captain Hibert A. Cunningham was uneven at best. As the ranking officer of any unit, Hibe was probably in it over his head. Cunningham's slow-moving four companies of about one-hundred men did manage to capture two of the guns of the Nineteenth Indiana Light Artillery, but only because Cunningham's troops had fallen so far behind Wall's troops.

With only fourteen officers and men engaged—only nine of who fought together under Second Lieutenant Bryant W. Hudgens—G Company cannot be evaluated as a combat unit at Perryville. That half of the regiment with Dr. Wall, however, did quite well as a fighting force, consistently coming up on the left in support of the Sixteenth Tennessee, Donelson's only front-line unit to participate in the deadly action at the rail fence against the Thirty-Third Ohio Infantry. Just as at Shiloh, Sergeant Metcalf and Private Blankenship were heroes of the regimental color-guard, which advanced with Wall. These two Carbondale Confederates should be considered the top enlisted men of Brooks' thirty-four Southern Illinois recruits. After Perryville Brooks expressed little confidence in Cunningham. At this time Metcalf observed that Brooks and Cunningham, previously personal friends, were not getting along.

After Shiloh, Cheatham was angry about the Confederate withdrawal and wrote only an abbreviated battle report for army headquarters. After Perryville, he was even more angry about the Confederate withdrawal and refused to provide any battle report for the army, or for the war department, or for the newspapers, or for anyone. Fortunately the general wrote extensively about the operations of his division at Perryville following the war. Several of his materials, published and unpublished, are used in the text.

The reason generally given for General Buell's not hearing the guns at

Perryville is a natural phenomenon known as "acoustic shadow," which supposedly muffled sounds coming from the battlefield. Given the number of scouts available to his Western commander, President Lincoln was not all that impressed with this theory and fired Buell.

1. Grimsley, Mark. "A Wade in the High Tide at Perryville," *CWTI*, Nov/Dec, 1992, p. 22; Kennedy, Frances H., Editor. *The Civil War Battlefield Guide*, p. 92.

2. Gilbert, Charles C. "Bragg's Kentucky Campaign," *Southern Bivouac (SB)*, vol. 1, p. 432; Suhr, Robert Collins, "Kentucky Neutrality Threatened," *America's Civil War (ACW)*, July, 1992, p. 22, p. 24.

3. McWhiney, Grady. "Controversy in Kentucky: Braxton Bragg's Campaign of 1862," *Civil War History (CWH)*, vol. 6, pp. 5–42.

4. Cheatham, B. Franklin. "General Donelson's Brigade at Perryville and Murfreesboro," Manuscript Division, L of C; Horn, *Tennesseeans in the Civil War*, "Thirty-Eighth Tennessee Infantry Regiment," vol. 1, p. 257.

5. Johnson, R. U. and C. C. Buel, Editors. "The Opposing Forces at Perryville," *BL*, vol. 3, pp. 29–30.

6. Wheeler, Joseph. "Bragg's Invasion of Kentucky," *BL*, vol. 3, pp. 1–25.

7. *Louisville Daily Journal*, October 4, 1862.

8. Hofendorfer, Kenneth A. *Perryville: Battle for Kentucky*, p. 95.

9. Ibid., pp. 98–9.

10. Kennedy, *Battlefield Guide*, pp. 94–5.

11. AOR, Serial No. 22, pp. 1088–90 (Bragg).

12. Ibid., p. 1038 (McCook).

13. Ibid., p. 1110 (Polk).

14. Ibid., p. 1092 (Bragg).

15. Ibid., p. 1092–3 (Polk); Cheatham, "Battle of Perryville," *SB*, vol. 2, p. 704; Cheatham, "General Donelson's Brigade at Perryville and Murfreesboro," Manuscripts Division, L of C; Horn, *Tennesseeans in the Civil War*, "First Tennessee Light Artillery Regiment," vol. 1, p. 122, and "Captain Marshall T. Polk's Tennessee Light Artillery Company," p. 145.

16. AOR, Serial No. 22, p. 1121 (Hardee); Finley, Luke W., "Battle of Perryville," *SHSP*, vol. 30, pp. 238–40.

17. AOR, Serial No. 22, pp. 1110–11 (Polk) and pp. 1038–9

(McCook); Claiborne, Thomas, "Battle of Perryville," *CV*, vol. 16, p. 225.

18. Cheatham, "General Donelson's Brigade at Perryville and Murfreesboro," Manuscripts Division, L of C; Horn, *Tennesseeans in the Civil War*, "Fifteenth Tennessee Infantry," vol. 1, p. 207; Lindsley, *Military Annals of Tennessee: Confederate*, Carroll, "Fifteenth Tennessee Infantry," p. 333 and Dillard, H. H., "Sixteenth Tennessee Infantry," pp. 340–1.

19. CSR, TSLA for S. Blankenship, F. Metcalf; Metcalf, October 22, 1900. letter to Dickinson.

20. Dyer, *Compendium*, vol. 3, p. 1512; Hofendorfer, *Perryville*, pp. 204–5; Lindsley, *Military Annals of Tennessee: Confederate*; Dillard, "Sixteenth Tennessee Infantry," p. 341.

21. AOR, Serial No. 22, p. 1111 (Polk); Cheatham, "Battle of Perryville," *SB*, vol. 2, pp. 704–5.

22. AOR, Serial No. 22, p. 1040 (McCook) and p. 1049 (L. Harris); Cheatham, "General Donelson's Brigade at Perryville and Murfreesboro," Manuscripts Division, L of C; CSR, TSLA for S. Blankenship, F. Metcalf; Polk, Leonidas, "The Right Wing at Perryville," DuPont Library, University of the South.

23. AOR, Serial No. 22, p. 1049 (L. Harris); *Louisville Daily Journal*, October 14, 1862.

24. Dyer, *Compendium*, "2nd Regiment," vol. 3, p. 1496; Hofendorfer, *Perryville*, p. 208; *Louisville Times*, October 15, 1862.

25. AOR, Serial No. 22, p. 1044 (Rousseau) and p. 1081 (Sheridan); Hicken, *Illinois in the Civil War*, p. 102.

26. AOR, Serial No. 22, pp. 1041–2 (McCook); Metcalf, October 22, 1900 letter to Dickinson.

27. Cheatham, "Battle of Perryville," *SB*, vol. 2, p. 705; Lindsley, *Military Annals of Tennessee: Confederate*, Dillard, "Sixteenth Tennessee Infantry," p. 341; Porter, George C., "Tennessee Infantry Regiments: The Fifteenth," Document No. 39, TSLA.

28. AOR, Serial No. 22, p. 1050 (L. Harris)

29. Ibid., pp. 1155–6 (Starkweather); *Chicago Daily Tribune*, October 15, 1862; CSR, TSLA for H.A. Cunningham, J. M. Wall; Hofendorfer, *Perryville*, pp. 245–7.

30. AOR, Serial No. 22, p. 1111 (Polk); *Report of the Illinois Adjutant*

General, vol. 2, p. 325; Wright, J. Montgomery, "Notes of a Union Staff Officer at Perryville," *BL,* vol. 3, pp. 60–1.

31. Polk, "The Right Wing at Perryville," DuPont Library, University of the South; Tapp, Hamberton, "The Battle of Perryville, 1862," *Filson Club History Quarterly* (Louisville), vol. 9, p. 181.

32. Horn, *Tennesseeans in the Civil War,* "Fifteenth Tennessee Infantry Regiment," vol. 1, p. 207; Livermore, *Numbers and Losses,* p. 95.

33. CSR, TSLA for S. Blankenship, A. J. Dillard, J. Finnegan, F. Metcalf.

34. Ibid., for J. Ables, T. Brooks, J. M. Wall.

Postscript

1. CSR, TSLA for T. Brooks, R. D. Fraser, R. C. Tyler, J. M. Wall.
2. Ibid., for W. B. Bate, T. Brooks, R. D. Fraser, T.B. Smith, R. M. Tankesley, R. C. Tyler, J. M. Wall.
3. Ibid., for J. Ables.
4. Ibid., for H. A. Cunningham; Simon, John Y., *Thirty-First Illinois* (Foreward), p. X.
5. CSR, TSLA for A. G. Morris, F. Ogle.
6. Ibid., for J. M. Wall; Chickamauga National Military Park Document Nos. 3008 and 3010; Kennesaw Mountain National Military Park Document Nos. 2068 and 2069.
7. CSR, TSLA for E. Gomand.
8. Ibid., for S. H. Graham.
9. Ibid., for S. Blankenship.
10. Ibid., for T. Brooks, B. W. Hudgens, R. Mullens.
11. Allardice. "Out of the Shadows," *CWTI,* Jan/Feb, 1995, pp. 58–60.

Epilogue

1. Cunningham, S. A. "Disastrous Campaign in Tennessee," *CV,* vol.

12, pp. 338–41; Horn, *Tennesseeans in the Civil War*, "Forty-First Tennessee Infantry," vol. 1, p. 263; Metcalf, Frank, "The Illinois Confederate Company," *CV*, vol. 16, pp. 224–5; Sword, Wiley, *Embrace An Angry Wind*, pp. 210–11.

2. *Western Kentucky Weekly Gazette* (Paducah), October 7, 1917.

3. Elliott, C. M. and L. A. Moxley, Editors. *The Tennessee Civil War Veterans Questionnaires*, vol. 2, p. 808.

Bibliography

Unpublished Materials

Allardice, Bruce. February 14, 1995, letter and subsequent interview with author in regards to Charles Montgomery Carroll, William Henry Carroll, Robert Dudley Fraser, and Robert Charles Tyler.

Bearss, Edwin C. "Artillery Study." Shiloh National Military Park Library. Shiloh, Tennessee.

Bell, Tyree H. "Report of the Battle of Belmont." Morris Library, Southern Illinois University. Carbondale, Illinois.

Cheatham, Benjamin Franklin. "General Donelson's Brigade at Perryville and Murfreesboro." Manuscripts Division, Library of Congress, Washington, D.C.

Cunningham, Hilbert G. July 7, 1995, letter to the author in regards to the Henry Cunningham Collection, including references to Captain Hibert A. Cunningham and Sergeant Frank Metcalf. Metropolis, Illinois.

Dosch, Donald F. "The Hornets Nest." Shiloh National Military Park Library. Shiloh, Tennessee.

Erwin, Milo. "Williamson County Illinois: Historical Essays." Illinois State Historical Library, Springfield, Illinois.

Hardee, William J. Letter to Mrs. Felicia Shover, April 9, 1862. Manuscripts Division, Library of Congress. Washington, D.C.

Illinois State Census, 1855, 1865, 1875. Illinois State Historical Library, Springfield, Illinois.

Johnson, Bushrod R. "Shiloh." Manuscripts Division, Library of Congress, Washington, D.C.

Kay, William. "The Sunken Road." Shiloh National Military Park Library, Shiloh, Tennessee.

Kentucky State Census, 1855, 1865. Kentucky State Library and Archives, Louisville, Kentucky.

Lake, Lewis F. "My War Service as a Member of Taylor's Battery, Company B, First Illinois Light Artillery." Illinois State Historical Library, Springfield, Illinois.

Metcalf, Frank. "Letters to Judge J. M. Dickinson, September 29, October 22, 1900." Henry Cunningham Collection, Paducah, Kentucky.

National Archives and Records Administration (NARA). Washington, D.C. Military Reference Branch, Confederate Record Group Number 109. Company G, Fifteenth Tennessee Infantry, C.S.A. Muster Rolls, (MR). Index Cards of Confederate Records (ICCR). Army of Tennessee Inspection Reports (ATIR).

Polk, Leonidas. "The Right Wing at Perryville." DuPont Library, University of the South, Sewanee, Tennessee.

Porter, George C. "Tennessee Confederate Regiments: The Fifteenth." Infantry Regimental Papers, Document Number 39. Tennessee State Library and Archives (TSLA), Nashville, Tennessee.

Schwartz, Adolphus. "The Battle of Belmont." Chicago Historical Society. Chicago, Illinois.

_____. "Biography of General John A. McClernand." Manuscript. 2 Volumes. Illinois State Historical Library, Springfield, Illinois.

Smith, Clifton H. "Letter to General P.G.T. Beauregard, August 5, 1880." Chicago Historical Society, Chicago, Illinois.

Tennessee State Census, 1855, 1865. Tennessee State Library and Archives (TSLA), Nashville, Tennessee.

Tennessee State Library and Archives (TSLA). Nashville, Tennessee. Company G, Fifteenth Tennessee Infantry, C.S.A. Confederate Military Service Records (CSR).

Tennessee State Library and Archives (TSLA). Nashville, Tennessee. Company G, Fifteenth Tennessee Infantry, C.S.A. Veterans Pension Application Numbers 3281 and 4551.

United States. Department of the Interior. National Park Service Center. Denver, Colorado. "Military Operations." Chickamauga and Chattanooga National Military Park Document Numbers 3008 and 3010.

_____. "Atlanta Campaign, 1863–64." Kennesaw Mountain National Military Park Document Numbers 2068 and 2069.

_____. "Troop Positions, First Day." Shiloh National Military Park Document Numbers 2064 and 2065.

_____. "Troop Movements, 1862–1863." Stones River National Military Park Document Numbers 3003 and 3006.

Yates, Richard. "May 15, 1861 letter to President Abraham Lincoln." John A. McClernand Collection. Illinois State Historical Library. Springfield, Illinois.

Government Publications

United States. Bureau of the Census. *Eighth Census of the United States, 1860* (statistical account taken from the census). 4 volumes. Washington, D.C., Government Printing Office. 1861–1862.

United States. Department of the Navy. *War of the Rebellion: Official Records of the Union and Confederate Navies* (NOR). 30 volumes and index. Washington, D.C., Government Printing Office. 1894–1927.

United States. War Department. *Official Military Atlas of the Civil War.* Washington, D.C., Government Printing Office. 1891–1896.

_____. *War of the Rebellion: Official Records of the Union and Confederate Armies* (AOR). 128 books and index. Government Printing Office, 1880–1901.

Newspapers

Cairo Argus

Cairo Democrat

Chicago Daily Tribune

The Courier-Journal [Louisville]

Daily Missouri Republican [St. Louis]

Illinois State Journal [Springfield]

Louisville Daily Journal

The Louisville Times

Memphis Daily Appeal

Nashville Banner

Nashville Dispatch

Nashville Union and American

New Orleans Daily Crescent

St. Louis Sunday Republican

Western Kentucky Weekly Gazette [Paducah]

Articles and Essays

Allardice, Bruce. "Out of the Shadows." (Robert C. Tyler) *Civil War Times Illustrated.* (January/February, 1995) pp. 27–9 and pp. 54–60.

Allen, Christopher J. "Devil's Own Day." (Shiloh) *America's Civil War.* (January, 1991), pp. 22–8.

Barnwell, Robert W. "The Battle of Belmont." *Confederate Veteran,* vol. 39, pp. 370–1.

Beauregard, P. G. T. "The Campaign of Shiloh." *Battles and Leaders of the Civil War,* vol. 1, pp. 569–93.

Buell, Don Carlos. "East Tennessee and the Campaign of Perryville." *Battles and Leaders of the Civil War,* vol. 3, pp. 31–51.

_____. "Shiloh Reviewed." *Battles and Leaders of the Civil War,* vol. 1, pp. 487–536.

Carnes, W. W. "In the Battle of Belmont." *Confederate Veteran,* vol. 39, pp. 369–70.

Carroll, Charles M. "Fifteenth Tennessee Infantry." From John B. Lindsley's Serial, *Military Annals of Tennessee: Confederate,* pp. 332–5.

Cartwell, J. M. "Witness to the Battle of Belmont." *Confederate Veteran,* vol. 16, p. 190.

Chalaron, J. A. "Battle Echoes from Shiloh." *Southern Historical Society Papers,* vol. 21, pp. 215–24.

Cheatham, Benjamin Franklin. "Battle of Perryville." *Southern Bivouac,* vol. 2, pp. 704–5.

Chisolm, A. R. "The Shiloh Battle Order and the Withdrawal Sunday Evening." *Battles and Leaders of the Civil War,* vol. 1, p. 606.

Claiborne, Thomas. "Battle of Perryville." *Confederate Veteran,* vol. 16, p. 225.

Connelly, Thomas Lawrence. "The Johnston Mystique." *Civil War Times Illustrated,* (February, 1967), p. 14.

Crooker, L. B. "Battle of Shiloh." *Manual of the Panorama of the Battle of Shiloh,* Chicago, 1885, pp. 1–15.

Cunningham, S. A. "Disastrous Campaign in Tennessee." *Confederate Veteran,* vol. 12, pp. 338–41.

Derry, Joseph Tyrone. "Battle of Shiloh." *Southern Historical Society Pa-*

pers, vol. 29, pp. 357–60.

Dickinson, J. M. "Secession Spirit (1861) in Illinois." *Confederate Veteran*, vol. 9, pp. 5–6.

Dillard, H. H. "Sixteenth Tennessee Infantry." From John B. Lindsley's Serial, *Military Annals of Tennessee: Confederate*, pp. 335–47.

Dinkens, James. "The Battle of Shiloh." *Southern Historical Society Papers*, vol. 31, pp. 298–320.

Ecelbarger, Gary L. "Shiloh: Where Death Knows No Distinction." *Civil War Society Magazine*, (April, 1995), pp. 66–9.

Eisenschiml, Otto. "Shiloh: The Blunders and The Blame." *Civil War Times Illustrated*, vol. 2, p. 6.

Ellertsen, Peter. "The Battle of Belmont and the Citizen Soldiers of the 27th Illinois Infantry." *Civil War Regiments: A Journal of the American Civil War*, vol. 3, no. 4, pp. 24–67.

Finley, Luke W. "Battle of Perryville." *Southern Historical Society Papers*, vol. 30, pp. 238–50.

Gilbert, Charles C. "Bragg's Kentucky Campaign." *Southern Bivouac*, vol. 1, p. 432.

_____. "On the Field at Perryville." *Battles and Leaders of the Civil War*, vol. 3, pp. 52–9.

Gleeson, Ed. "The Battle of Erin Hollow." *Dixie Liberator*, vol. 3, no. 1, pp. 18–22.

_____. "Sergeant John Condon: Tennessee Engineer." *Confederate Veteran*. May/June, 1991, pp. 16–23.

Grant, U. S. "The Battle of Shiloh." *Battles and Leaders of the Civil War*, vol. 1, pp. 465–86.

Grimsley, Mark. "A Wade in the High Tide at Perryville." *Civil War Times Illustrated*, (November/December, 1992), pp. 22–4.

Hay, Thomas Robson. "Braxton Bragg and the Southern Confederacy." *Georgia Historical Quarterly*, vol. 9, pp. 267–316.

Hickenlooper, Andrew. "The Battle of Shiloh." *Sketches of War History, 1861–1865. Military Order of the Loyal Legion of the United States, Ohio Commandery*, vol. 5, 1903.

Hubbard, G. H. "In the Battle of Belmont, Mo." *Confederate Veteran*, vol. 30, p. 459.

Johnson, Robert Underwood and Clarence Clough Buel, Editors. "The

Opposing Forces at Perryville." *Battles and Leaders of the Civil War*, vol. 3, pp. 29–30.

_____. The Opposing Forces at Shiloh." *Battles and Leaders of the Civil War*, vol. 1, pp. 537–9.

Johnson, Timothy D. "Benjamin Franklin Cheatham at Belmont." *Missouri Historical Review*, vol. 81, pp. 159–72.

Johnston, William Preston. "Albert Sidney Johnston at Shiloh." *Battles and Leaders of the Civil War*, vol. 1, pp. 540–68.

Jordan, Thomas. "Battle of Shiloh." *Southern Historical Society Papers*, vol. 16, pp. 297–318 and vol. 35, pp. 204–30.

_____. "Notes of a Confederate Staff Officer at Shiloh." *Battles and Leaders of the Civil War*, vol. 1, pp. 594–603.

Kegley, Tracy M. "Bushrod Rust Johnson: Soldier and Teacher." *Tennessee Historical Quarterly*, vol. 7, pp. 249–58.

Kurtz, Henry I. "The Battle of Belmont." *Civil War Times Illustrated*, vol. 3, pp. 18–24.

Lockett, S.H. "Surprise and Withdrawal at Shiloh." *Battles and Leaders of the Civil War*, vol. 1, pp. 604–6.

Mason, George. "Shiloh." *Sketches of War History, 1861–1865. Military Order of the Loyal Legion of the United States, Ohio Commandery*, vol. 1, 1891, pp. 98–101.

McDonough, James Lee. "Shiloh: The Hornets Nest." *Confederate Veteran*, January/February, 1987, pp. 14–18.

McWhiney, Grady. "Braxton Bragg and the Shiloh Campaign." *Tennessee Historical Quarterly*, vol. 21, pp. 19–30.

_____. "Controversy in Kentucky: Braxton Bragg's Campaign of 1862." *Civil War History Magazine*, vol. 6, pp. 5–42.

Medlink, Robert W. "Skirmishing in Sherman's Front." (Shiloh) *Battles and Leaders of the Civil War*, vol. 1, p. 537.

Merrill, James. "Cairo, Illinois: Strategic Civil War River Port." *Journal of the Illinois State Historical Society*, vol. 76, no. 4 (Winter 1983), pp. 242–57.

Metcalf, Frank. "The Illinois Confederate Company." *Confederate Veteran*, vol. 16, pp. 224–5.

Polk, William M. "Army of the Mississippi Before Shiloh." *Southern Historical Society Papers*, vol. 8, pp. 457–63 and vol. 9, pp. 178–85.

_____. "General Polk and the Battle of Belmont." *Battles and Leaders of the Civil War*, vol. 1, pp. 348–57.

Ramage, James A. "The Wounded at Shiloh." *Civil War Society Magazine*, May/June, 1991, pp. 10–14 and pp. 44–5.

Ross, John Kelly, Jr. "Confederate Columbus: The Story of the Lady Polk." *Confederate Veteran*, September/October, 1990, pp. 6–10.

Ruggles, Daniel. "Notes on Shiloh." *Southern Historical Society Papers*, vol. 7, pp. 35–47 and vol. 9, pp. 49–63.

Sandridge, L. D. "The Battle of Shiloh." *Southern Historical Society Papers*, vol. 8, pp. 173–7.

Simon, John Y. "Civil War Comes to Williamson County." *Springhouse Magazine* (Herod, Illinois), vol. 8, no. 6 (December 1991), pp. 33–4.

_____. "Grant at Belmont." *Military Affairs Magazine*, vol. 45, pp. 161–6.

Singletary, Don. "The Battle of Belmont." *Confederate Veteran*, vol. 23, pp. 506–7.

Stillwell, Leander. "In the Ranks at Shiloh." *Journal of the Illinois State Historical Society*, vol. 15, pp. 460–76.

Stonesifer, Roy P. "Gideon Pillow: A Study in Egotism." *Tennessee Historical Quarterly*, vol. 25, pp. 340–50.

Suhr, Robert Collins. "Kentucky Neutrality Threatened." *America's Civil War*, July, 1992, pp. 22–8.

Tapp, Hamberton. "The Battle of Perryville, 1862." *Filson Club (Louisville) Historical Quarterly*, vol. 9, pp. 158–81.

Taylor, William. "About the Battle of Belmont." *Confederate Veteran*, vol. 16, pp. 345–6.

Walke, Henry. "The Gunboats at Belmont and Fort Henry." *Battles and Leaders of the Civil War*, vol. 1, pp. 360–1.

Walker, Peter Franklin. "Building a Tennessee Army: Autumn, 1861." *Tennessee Historical Quarterly*, vol. 16, pp. 99–116.

Wallace, Lewis. "The March of Lew Wallace's Division to Shiloh." *Battles and Leaders of the Civil War*, vol. 1, pp. 607–10.

Weinert, Richard P. "The Little-Known Story of the Illinois Confederates." *Civil War Times Illustrated*, vol. 2 (1961), pp. 44–5.

Wheeler, Joseph. "The Battle of Shiloh." *Southern Historical Society Papers*, vol. 24, pp. 119–31.

_____. "Bragg's Invasion of Kentucky." *Battles and Leaders of the Civil War*, vol. 3, pp. 1–25.

Wilds, George B. "Battle of Belmont, Mo." *Confederate Veteran*, vol. 32, pp. 485–6.

Wright, J. Montgomery. "Notes of a Union Staff Officer at Perryville." *Battles and Leaders of the Civil War*, vol. 3, pp. 60–1.

Wright, Marcus Joseph. "Battle of Belmont." *Southern Historical Society Papers*, vol. 16, pp. 69–82 and vol. 32, pp. 122–33.

Books

Allardice, Bruce. *More Generals In Gray*. Baton Rouge: Louisiana State University Press, 1995.

Allen, John W. *Legends and Lore of Southern Illinois*. Carbondale: Southern Illinois University Press, 1963.

Alvord, Clarence W. *The Centennial History of Illinois*. 5 volumes. Springfield: Illinois Centennial Commission Publishers, 1919.

Bateman, Newton and Paul Selby. Editors. *Historical Encyclopedia of Illinois*. Chicago: Munsell Publishers, 1900.

Boatner, Mark M. III. Editor. *Civil War Dictionary*. New York: David McKay, 1959.

Campaigns of the Civil War. 16 volumes. New York: Charles Scribner's Sons, 1881–1882.

Catton, Bruce. *Grant Moves South*. Boston: Little, Brown and Company, 1960.

_____. *Never Call Retreat*. Garden City, New York: Doubleday and Company, Inc., 1965.

_____. *This Hallowed Ground*. Garden City, New York: Doubleday and Company, Inc., 1956.

Cist, Henry M. *Army of the Cumberland*. New York: Charles Scribner's Sons, 1882.

Cole, Arthur Charles. *The Era of the Civil War*. 5 volumes. Springfield: Illinois Centennial Commission Publishers, 1919.

Confederate Veteran. 40 volumes and 3-volume index. Nashville: edited and published by the *Confederate Veteran Magazine*, 1893–1932.

Connelly, Thomas Lawrence. *Army of the Heartland: Army of Tennessee, 1861–1862.* Reprint. Baton Rouge: Louisiana State University Press, 1988.

_____. *Autumn of Glory: Army of Tennessee, 1862–1865.* Reprint. Baton Rouge: Louisiana State University Press, 1988.

_____. *Civil War Tennessee.* Reprint. Baton Rouge: Louisiana State University Press, 1988.

Connelly, Thomas W. *History of the Seventieth Ohio Regiment.* Cincinnati: Peak Publishers, 1902.

Cox, Jacob D. *Atlanta.* New York: Charles Scribner's Sons, 1882.

Cummings, Charles M. *Yankee Quaker Confederate General: The Curious Career of Bushrod Rust Johnson.* Rutherford, New Jersey: Associated University Presses, 1971.

Davidson, Alexander and Bernard Stuvé. *A Complete History of Illinois from 1673 to 1884.* Springfield: H. W. Rokker, 1884.

Davis, William C. *Breckinridge: Statesman, Soldier, Symbol.* Baton Rouge: Louisiana State University Press, 1986.

_____. Editor. *Confederate General.* 6 volumes. Washington, D.C.: National Historical Publication, 1991–1992.

Dawson, George Francis. *Life and Services of General John A. Logan: Soldier and Statesman.* Chicago: Belford, Clarke, and Company, 1887.

Drake, Edwin L. Editor. *Annals of the Army of Tennessee.* Nashville: A. D. Haynes, 1878–1879.

Duke, John K. *History of the 53rd Ohio Volunteer Infantry.* Portsmouth, Ohio: Blade Printing Company, 1900.

Dyer, Frederick H. *Compendium of the War of Rebellion.* 3 volumes. Des Moines, Iowa: Dyer Publishing Company, 1908.

Eddy, Thomas Mears. *The Patriotism of Illinois.* 2 volumes. Chicago: Clarke and Company, 1865–1866.

Eisenschiml, Otto. *The Story of Shiloh.* Chicago: Norman Press, 1946.

Elliot, Colleen Morse and Louise Armstrong Moxley. Editors. *Tennessee Civil War Veterans Questionnaires.* 5 volumes. Nashville: Southern Historical Society Press, 1922.

Erwin, Milo. *The History of Williamson County Illinois.* Macon, Illinois: Macon Press, 1876.

Evans, Clement A. Editor. *Confederate Military History.* 17 volumes. Atlanta: Confederate Publishing Company, 1899.

Faust, Patricia L. Editor. *Historical Times Illustrated: Encyclopedia of the Civil War.* New York: Harper and Row, 1986.

Foote, Shelby. *The Civil War: A Narrative, Fort Sumter to Perryville.* Reprint. New York: Vantage Books, 1986.

_____. *The Civil War: A Narrative, Fredericksburg to Meridian.* Reprint. New York: Vantage Books, 1986.

_____. *The Civil War: A Narrative, Red River to Appomattox.* Reprint. New York: Vantage Books, 1986.

Force, M. F. *From Fort Henry to Corinth.* New York: Charles Scribner's Sons, 1881.

Fox, William F. *Regimental Losses in the Civil War.* Albany, New York: Albany Publishing Company, 1889.

Gleeson, Ed. *Rebel Sons of Erin: A Civil War Unit History of the Tenth Tennessee Infantry Regiment (Irish), Confederate States Volunteers.* Indianapolis: Guild Press of Indiana, 1993.

Greene, F. V. *The Mississippi.* New York: Charles Scribner's Sons, 1882.

Grant, U. S. *Personal Memoirs of U.S. Grant.* 2 volumes. New York: Charles L. Webster and Company, 1885-1886.

Hafendorfer, Kenneth A. *Perryville: Battle for Kentucky.* Louisville: K. H. Press, 1981.

Hicken, Victor. *Illinois in the Civil War.* Champaign-Urbana: University of Illinois Press, 1966.

Horn, Stanley F. *The Army of Tennessee.* Indianapolis: Bobbs-Merrill, 1941.

_____. Editor and Chairman, Civil War Centennial Commission. *Tennesseeans in the Civil War: A Military History of Confederate and Union Units With Available Rosters of Personnel.* 2 volumes. Knoxville: University of Tennessee Press, 1964–1965.

Hughes, Nathaniel C., Jr. *The Battle of Belmont: Grant Strikes South.* Chapel Hill: University of North Carolina Press, 1991.

_____. *General William J. Hardee, Old Reliable.* Baton Rouge: Louisiana State University Press, 1965.

Illinois Military Units in the Civil War. Springfield: edited and published by the Civil War Centennial Commission of Illinois, 1962.

Jamison, Matthew H. *Recollections of Army and Pioneer Life.* (Co. E, 10th

Illinois Infantry) Kansas City, Missouri: Hudson Press, 1911.

Johnson, Robert Underwood and Clarence Clough. Editors. *Battles and Leaders of the Civil War.* 4 volumes. New York: Century Magazine Publishers, 1887–1889.

Johnston, William Preston. *The Life of General Albert Sidney Johnston.* New York: D. Appleton and Company, 1874.

Jones, James P. *John A. Logan and Southern Illinois in the Civil War Era.* Tallahassee: Florida State University Press, 1967.

Kennedy, Frances H. Editor. *Civil War Battlefield Guide.* Boston: Houghlin Mifflin, 1990.

Krenkel, John H. *Richard Yates: Civil War Governor.* Danville, Illinois: Interstate Printers and Publishers, 1966.

Lindsley, John B. Editor. *Military Annals of Tennessee: Confederate.* Nashville: J. B. Lindsley and Company Publishers, 1886.

Livermore, Thomas L. *Numbers and Losses in the Civil War.* Reprint. Bloomington: Indiana University Press, 1957.

Long, E. B. *Civil War Day By Day: An Almanac 1861–1865.* New York: Doubleday, 1971.

Losson, Christopher. *Tennessee's Forgotten Warriors: Frank Cheatham and His Confederate Division.* Knoxville: University of Tennessee Press, 1989.

McDonough, James Lee. *Shiloh: In Hell Before Dark.* Knoxville: University of Tennessee Press, 1977.

_____. *War in Kentucky: From Shiloh to Perryville.* Knoxville: University of Tennessee Press, 1994.

McWhiney, Grady. *Braxton Bragg and Confederate Defeat.* 2 volumes. New York: Columbia University Press, 1969.

Monaghan, Jay. *Swamp Fox of the Confederacy: The Life and Military Service of M. Jeff Thompson.* Tuscaloosa: University of Alabama Press, 1957.

Moses, John. *Illinois: Historical and Statistical.* 2 volumes. Chicago: Fergue Printing Company, 1889.

Nicolay, J. F. and John Hay. *Abraham Lincoln: A History.* 10 volumes. New York: The Century Company, 1890.

Parks, Joseph H. *General Leonidas Polk C.S.A.—The Fighting Bishop.* Baton Rouge: Louisiana State University Press, 1962.

Porter, James D. *Confederate Military History.* (Tennessee volume.) Atlanta: Confederate Publishing Company, 1899.

Rich, Joseph W. *The Battle of Shiloh.* Iowa City: State Historical Society of Iowa, 1911.

Roman, Alfred. *The Military Operations of General Beauregard in the War Between the States, 1861–1865.* 2 volumes. New York: Harper and Brothers, 1884.

Roller, David C. and Robert W. Twyman. Editors. *Encyclopedia of Southern History.* Baton Rouge: Louisiana State University Press, 1979.

Sherman, W. T. *Personal Memoirs of W. T. Sherman.* New York: D. Appleton and Company, 1875.

Sifakis, Stewart. *Compendium of the Confederate Armies: Florida and Arkansas.* New York: Facts on File Inc., 1992.

_____. *Compendium of the Confederate Armies: Tennessee.* New York: Facts on File Inc., 1992.

Smith, George W. *A History of Southern Illinois.* 3 volumes. Chicago: Munsell Publishers, 1912.

Southern Bivouac. 6 volumes. Louisville: edited and published by the Kentucky branch of the Southern Historical Society, 1882–1887.

Southern Historical Society Papers. 38 volumes. Richmond: edited and published by the Virginia branch of the Southern Historical Society, 1876–1913.

Steele, Matthew F. *American Campaigns.* Washington, D.C.: United States Infantry Association, 1922.

Street, James Jr. *The Struggle for Tennessee: Tupelo to Stones River.* Alexandria, Virginia: Time-Life Books, 1990.

Sword, Wiley. *Embrace An Angry Wind: The Confederacy's Last Hurrah: Spring Hill, Franklin, and Nashville.* Columbus: The General's Books, 1994.

_____. *Shiloh: Bloody April.* Dayton: Morningside Bookstore, 1974.

Thompson, Ed Porter. *History of the Orphan Brigade 1861–1865.* Louisville: Charles T. Dearing Press, 1898.

Vance, J. W. Editor. *Report of the Adjutant General of the State of Illinois.* 8 volumes. Springfield: H. W. Rokker, 1886.

Warner, Ezra J. *Generals in Blue.* Baton Rouge: Louisiana State University Press, 1964.

_____. *Generals in Gray.* Baton Rouge: Louisiana State University Press, 1959.

Way, Virgil and Isaac H. Elliot. *History of the Thirty-First Regiment Illinois Volunteer Infantry in the Civil War.* Gibson City, Illinois: published by the Regimental Association, 1902.

Wilson, Ephraim A. *Memoirs of the War.* (Co. G, 10th Illinois Infantry) Cleveland: W. M. Boyne Company, 1893.

Wright, Marcus Joseph. *Tennessee in the War, 1861–1865.* New York: A. Lee Publishing Company, 1908.

Index

NOTE: An asterisk (*) after a number indicates that a photo appears on that page.

With *Illinois Rebels*, a unit history of G Company of the Fifteenth Tennessee Infantry, historian Ed Gleeson continues his research into atypical Confederates, an ongoing project that began with his first title, *Rebel Sons of Erin*, a unit history of the Tenth Tennessee Infantry (Irish).

A resident of the Chicago suburb of Oak Lawn, Gleeson's Confederate ancestors were Irish-born Tennesseans. He is currently the commander of the Illinois division of the International Order of the Sons of Confederate Veterans, with the state organization now boasting five "camps" (chapters) throughout the "Land of Lincoln." He also holds membership in the Blue and Gray Education Society, the National Civil War Society, and the Chicago Historical Society. Besides his writing, Gleeson has also conducted various special research projects, including a report for Chicago's Oakwoods Cemetery of the 4,039 Camp Douglas prisoners buried there.